Stairway to Earth

29 September 2014

For Andy —

Here's to the future of books!

All best,

Bill

P.S.... and to future adventures in rafting!

Stairway to Earth

How to Write a Serious Book

—⚬—

Bill Birchard

BIRCHARD BOOKS

AMHERST, NEW HAMPSHIRE

OTHER BOOKS BY BILL BIRCHARD

Merchants of Virtue

Nature's Keepers

The One-Minute Meditator
WITH DAVID NICHOL MD

Counting What Counts
WITH MARC EPSTEIN

Appalachian Trail Design, Construction, and Maintenance
WITH ROBERT PROUDMAN

"The art of writing is the art of applying the seat of the pants to the seat of the chair."

~MARY HEATON VORSE
SUFFRAGETTE, JOURNALIST, NOVELIST, SINGLE MOM 1874–1966

Contents

Preface

Before You Start

As I was preparing to write my first book, I was more than excited. The prospect of producing something that would go on a bookstore shelf—why, the idea of fulfilling that ambition was uplifting. Maybe you are buoyed by the same prospect—and the added prospect of your book appearing on people's computers, e-book readers, and smart phones. A book with your name on it can return handsome rewards.

But before going farther, let me tell you a story. When I decided to kick off work on my first book, I stopped by the Boston office of a magazine editor I worked with. She warned me against it. "A book will tear your heart out," she said. She had written one herself. The memories still seemed to pain her. I sensed she was trying to save me from myself.

Of course, I didn't listen.

Nor would most people. After all, writing a book is a preeminent mark of accomplishment. I was determined to do it. But sure enough, my book was a trial I'll never forget—I still feel drained by the thought of it. For days at a time, I rose at 5:00 a.m. and wrote until 6:00 p.m. I despaired at all the paper, at the endless tangles in my logic, at the relentlessness of having to produce so much text.

When people tell me they want to write a book, I encourage them. It's a wonderful ambition. But I often recite my editor's line. She knew far better than I how people like me make a hasty assumption: A book is no more than a big version of a small article—if you can pen an article in a few weeks, you can crank out a manuscript in a few months.

But a seventy-five-thousand-word book is not like an article—no more than a dinner for two is like a banquet for one hundred. Even if you are adept at the former, you may be entirely out of your depth with the latter. Compared to magazine articles, a book calls on you to focus for so much longer. To master ideas that force you to stretch your mind so much farther. To execute a plan complicated enough that you just can't hold the whole thing in your head.

When you learn to craft a superb manuscript—and learn to control the process—nothing could be more gratifying. But when a book project isn't going well, you can slide into a state of disorientation. You can feel like you can't touch solid ground. I know the feeling. Intellectual vertigo wipes out your sense of judgment. And you yearn for a set of clear steps on which to reestablish your footing.

Stairway to Earth provides those steps. It equips you not only with thinking guidelines but organizational tools. All you need is a few hours—about the time it takes to watch a ballgame or movie—to read the Stairway steps, learn the book-writing process, and spare yourself agony later.

Perhaps you're already a writer. Or a teacher, professor, consultant, or other educator. Or an executive, manager, engineer, physician, lawyer, scientist, or other professional. No matter; if you're reading this book, I assume you share the ambition to publish a volume stocked by your favorite booksellers.

Your reasons may vary. Perhaps you want to advance your career, solidify your authority, build your brand, or earn the imprimatur of a publisher. Or perhaps you are simply smitten by the desire to share your wisdom with others, reveal insights, or create a legacy. A book can do all of these things—but only if you have a way to make them happen.

Stairway to Earth is that way.

But before you proceed, ask this question: Are you really ready to write a book? Once you make a commitment to dive into the publishing process—especially if you crow about it to your friends—you'll find it hard to turn back. I advise you not to plunge ahead until you're feeling fit to swim through the surf.

The following is a self-test to gauge your readiness. Rate yourself on a scale of one to ten:

1. Do I believe passionately in my book's message?

    10   I believe it in my heart and gut.

    1   I find it interesting.

2. Does my message reflect me as a person?

    10   It embodies my personal and professional philosophy.

    1   It reflects an interesting worldview.

3. Can I commit the time to complete the book?

    10   I have fifteen hundred hours of work time to commit.

    1   I have a few nights and a few weekends, perhaps twenty hours a month.

4. Do I have a core book-reading audience that cares about my message?

    10   Every professional in my field wants this book.

    1   I'm unsure, but I think a lot of people would benefit from the book.

5. If the book doesn't sell well, can I risk losing the money I spent writing and promoting it?

    10   I don't need to make money on the book.

    1   I need to earn the equivalent of a full salary.

6. Will my book be relevant upon publication—two years from now?

    10   My book taps into a perennial or rapidly growing trend.

    1   I'm not sure my book will be relevant in a year or two.

7. Does my book idea stand out from similar ones?

    10   I can tell you ten ways my book is unlike others.

    1   My book is just like others, but it will be a lot better.

8. Do I understand how to develop and write a book-length manuscript?

    10   I understand the steps in book development.

    1   I don't know the steps, but I'm sure I can do it.

9. Am I willing to make personal sacrifices to get the book done?

    10   My friends and family will gladly support my absence.

    1   My family and friends take priority over everything else.

10. Do I have a way to market my book?

    10   I host a radio talk show and run a public speaking and seminar series.

    1   I don't have any professional network to tap.

Now tally your score. Did you get a seventy or higher? If so, you're probably ready—ready to fulfill your ambition to write a book with handsome rewards. If not, decide for yourself if you need to think and prepare more. Maybe your idea needs more honing. Maybe you can't give up the family time until your kids get a year or two older.

Once you're ready, once you are confident you have the passion and time and commitment, you can embark in earnest on a gratifying, if challenging, journey to publication. The Stairway to Earth will guide you on your way—and allow you to put your heart into a book without putting your heart on the line.

Introduction

STEP BY STEP

Stairway to Earth lays out a systematic method for writing a serious nonfiction book. It takes you each step of the way from the exhilarating "aha" of an idea to the satisfying delivery of a final manuscript. It covers not just obvious tasks, but the hardest tasks, in what can otherwise be a trying, solitary effort. In the end, it guides you to the hallowed ground of authorship.

Many books set out to explain the A to Z of publishing. That's a tall order. They invariably have to leave a lot out. This book focuses on the tough part of book creation: the prewriting and writing steps. It covers the creative, thinking-intensive phases, where many people, even professional writers like me, can struggle to get their writing legs under them.

The first half of the book, the Stairway to Earth, shows how to get out of the clouds and down to earth. It includes eight chapters, which explain how to shape the message, fashion the argument, differentiate your treatment, inventory the content, organize a thematic outline, learn elements of craft, create a publishing game plan, and develop a work program. If you follow all of them, you end up with an irresistible book proposal ready to sell to a publisher.

I named the book after this first phase because I felt it deserved the most explanation. For one thing, the process of early development takes some of the hardest thinking and gives authors some of the worst headaches. For another, it remains among the most misunderstood, confusing, and poorly executed parts of book creation.

The second half of the book, the "Road to Publication," shows how to turn the proposal into a manuscript. It comprises six chapters, which explain how to retool the argument, complete the research, draft the chapters, frame the book with a preface and/or introduction and epilogue, edit the text, solicit feedback, and rewrite, rewrite, and rewrite again. When you finish with this work, you're ready to deliver a superb manuscript to your editor.

Together, the two parts of the book offer a handy guide for all writers—novice and professional—because the fourteen steps covered provide an answer to a critical question writers face nearly every day: How do I structure my work—structure it so I can proceed without hitting dead ends, making false starts, and swerving into a writing wilderness?

Put another way: How do I most efficiently draft a superb manuscript when faced with a bewildering array of decisions about treatment, positioning, logic, organization, structure, and wordsmithing?

The answer is that you need not just a stepwise process but one that adheres to a simple principle: To produce a large written work, you have to produce a lot of small ones along the way. This may seem blindingly obvious. Just as artists prepare a series of visual "studies" before executing a major work, book authors should prepare a series of successively more complex written studies before executing their manuscript.

The small documents give you time to think, research, explore, shape, practice, and perfect thoughts and language. You get your mind and words in line before you get your writing on track for publication. And when you work this way, you create a paper trail that both documents your work and provides a springboard for further progress.

The side benefit to a paper trail is that you have a way to readily gauge how far you've come. For weeks you may have no manuscript to show for yourself. But your many work-in-process documents confirm that you're blasting by one mileage marker after another on the way to publication. You can move forward steadily because you're not missing deadlines, and you're developing your book with confidence.

I have written this book mainly for people doing "concept" books—books about current affairs, science, business, management, self-help, how-to, and so on. But the process applies just as well to biography, history, and narrative nonfiction. All works of any great length—from giant research reports to PhD theses—require the assembly of carefully crafted building blocks to make them happen.

The beauty of the Stairway to Earth process is that it forces you to engage in the full range of thinking needed before you get to the manuscript. You brainstorm, journal, prototype, draft, test, and refine language—before you face the screen with a deadline to produce something publishable. In this way, your pile of developmental documents yields another wonderful side benefit: It helps you dodge writer's block.

The method in this book stems from my own experience. I have refined the approach while writing five books under my own byline, ghostwriting five books (including the draft of a best seller), and coaching authors in writing their own books. My experience spans more than twenty years—two decades of applying the seat of my pants to the seat of the chair.

One of my clients refers to the Stairway to Earth process as a way to "engineer" a manuscript. It took me a bit of time to get used to that idea, but he was right. Writing a book with control requires sticking to a critical path. It demands adhering to a schedule with milestones. It moves forward only with the production of a trail of "deliverables." It follows principles that, as in the best of engineering, build quality in at every stage.

Many people think of writing as an art. But writing a serious nonfiction book depends on applying a logical method for the rational left brain to follow, while giving the creative right brain guardrails within which to work. A measure of art is needed, but art won't get you across the finish line.

In my experience, the craft of writing a book calls for a number of engineering-like habits. Three deserve mention up front. The first is "pre-thinking." As with so much of life, the seeds of creativity germinate slowly. Before you start putting words to an idea, plant some of the emerging particulars in your mind. Give them time to sprout. If you have to write on Monday, tuck a few thoughts into the soil of your forebrain on Friday.

A second required habit is iteration. Although in outline the writing process proceeds in a fixed sequence, in practice you often move ahead two steps and back one before advancing to a third. Just as an oil painter reworks a canvas many times, you will go over and over your messages and argument and structure and text.

A third is a caveat. Although you have to iterate, you also have to organize your work to minimize the total number of iterations. The more revisions you make, the less you retain "fresh eyes." During every round of revisions, your perspective as a self-editor erodes. Eventually it erodes to zero. When this happens, you cease to have the capability to self-edit.

One of the ways to minimize your iterations is to start with a solid first draft. If, on a scale of 1 to 10, you want to get to an outstanding final draft, you can't start with a number 3. You have to start with at least a number 7. If you write a 7—and then set it aside—you can often loft it to a 9 on the next edit, and then to a 10 on the final edit.

Beware of sitting down and writing your first draft by simply letting thoughts pour out. Recognize that once you commit ideas to the screen, they establish tenure, and in time you'll have trouble recognizing the bad ones and giving them the boot. You need to be wary of getting comfortable with your own overwrought prose, poor word choice, and tangled logic.

In football terms, this is your challenge: Get enough yardage down the field on the kickoff that you can get the ball the rest of the way on four downs. In other words, don't write your first draft until you think you can do a good job. And try not to repeatedly reread between drafts. This is what I call the "Conservation of Freshness" principle.

A final few notes: First, once you learn the process, you may think the task of writing will be easy—that you will have weeks of fun writing. I wish this were true. But if so, books wouldn't have the value and cachet they do. Even with this process, writing your book will demand hard work. You will still have to keep your chin up during days when you're wondering why the heck you ever got started.

Second, I promise a lot, but not the ultimate success of your book. In books, as in movies, nobody can guarantee a box-office hit. Even if you manage to produce a superb product, achieving commercial success remains tough. If nothing else, you face the challenge of all retailers in today's world: Very little sells well without publicity, marketing, and of course, luck.

What I can say is that, if you follow the process in this book, you will come out of the clouds, step down to earth, and at least hit the ground running. You will have the system, the tools, and the capability to produce an authoritative, handsome book. You will have then given yourself a shot at publishing's many rewards—robust sales, well-earned recognition, and an impact on the world around you that other achievements can't match.

PART 1

The Stairway to Earth

CHAPTER 1

RIGHT MESSAGE

A songwriter friend once told me the trick to writing a great song: "First come up with the title. From the title, everything just flows." I thought about this from the point of view of books, and I wondered: If you can come up with just the right title, can the book just flow?

I decided the answer could be yes, if the title captured the message *exactly*. That's because the message is the refrain that repeats throughout the book, and a great refrain is what makes a song—and any written work—memorable.

The thought of this gave me a jolt. Whoa! Maybe all the pain I had experienced as an author was just from my lack of knowing the right tricks. But the thought quickly passed. Assuming you'll be this lucky is like assuming you can whistle with perfect pitch, when you've never whistled before. True enough, if you're a natural, you may get it right. But otherwise you'll probably blow off-key.

Fact is, most of us aren't naturals. So I advise authors, before anything else, to invest time in developing a message in a systematic way. The right message—and title—may come easily, but they usually come only after a process of creative struggling.

Why is a message so important as a first step? Because the secret of quality writing is focus, and developing a message forces you to narrow your focus before broadening your research and writing. If you start with too broad a focus, you risk letting your writing project spin out of control. Losing control will cost you time and energy. It may cost you money. It may even cost you your sanity.

So what is a "message"? Let's start with what it isn't. It's not a subject or topic. It's not "what the book is about." It's what the book says. It's the point the reader takes away and tells friends about. Think about it as the "aha," or the central insight. It is that refrain that appears throughout the book.

You could also call it the "thesis" or the "theme," but those words can evoke angst. They will remind you of papers and dissertations in school. Who wants to be reminded of late nights and imperious teachers. Of whistling in the dark when you weren't really sure what your song was.

To be sure, the teachers were often right. They said you needed to start with a statement that expresses your point in a compact sentence. I agree. And you want it to be catchy if you can, even turn a few heads. And what's more, you want to capture some magic in a title.

Starting on the message

Before you start popping words on paper, reflect a bit on where you're going. First, is your message emerging in a way that expresses your passion? Books are exhausting projects, even when they go well. If you're in for the long haul, you have to have a passion for your idea. Do you care so much that once someone gets you talking you have trouble shutting up? Does a current of enthusiasm course through your veins? No passion, no energy, no follow-through.

Next, have you thoroughly thought through your goals? Do you want to make a name for yourself? Disseminate your ideas? Build your business's brand? Secure a step to tenure? Make money? Goals shape your writing at every step. So write them down. And be specific—and honest. Why are you going to all this trouble? If you're going to exhaust yourself, by all means choose a worthy reason.

Third, ask yourself, Who are my readers? Are they forty-somethings in sweat suits at casino tables? Sixty-somethings trading stocks in their pajamas? Young-buck engineers out to save the world? What do they care about? Worry about? Want insights about? Need solutions to? How do they like to be spoken to?

Paint a mental picture of these readers. Or better yet, cut a good likeness out of a magazine and tape it over your desk.

And don't even think about your audience as "everyone." Readers have so many choices in our multiplying media age. How will you shape your message so you have a loyal group of readers who will stick with you? When the amphitheater empties out, who will linger to ask you questions after the show? These are your *core* readers, and you need to please them first.

Finally, ask yourself if your subject or message or theme reflects who you are. Does it stem from your personality, preferences, and strengths? You will inevitably bake into your writing a bit of yourself, even if your subject is dry and technical. If you're not kneading into the dough the real you, you'll know your work lacks flavor and depth, and so will your readers.

You're now ready to work with words. I recommend three tasks in this first step in the Stairway to Earth process:

CIRCLING

AMENDING

FIRMING

Circling

Ever notice that, at dusk, the most striking element in a landscape often pops up in your peripheral vision? That has something to do with the anatomy of the eye. (Better to see predators with.) The same thing is true about the most striking elements in a message. They often emerge from the periphery of your thinking. They come out of nowhere.

That's why it usually pays to resist the temptation to start work on a message by focusing on what's front and center. Better to circle the subject like a thief casing a robbery site. Don't act greedily, dashing for the jewels on the first pass. Explore the outside of the building. Look for a backdoor entrance. Make sure you haven't missed valuables hidden in the shadows.

I'm a big proponent of using a pencil and paper for circling. A pencil gives your work a relaxed feel compared to when you're punching words into a computer. You can be playful, use a lot of arrows, carets, and sketches. There's no such thing as a mistake. You remain noncommittal, quixotic, and have fun. The temporary—or tentative—nature of pencil on paper pushes your mind beyond the straight-and-narrow alleyway of designated lines of thinking. You can examine the full breadth of your topical territory, surface unverbalized thoughts, and shape new insights.

Here are some aids for circling:

— Browse books online: On amazon.com or bn.com, search for books like yours—and books you like. What messages do they explore? What language do they use?

— Check for trends: Go to sites like Google Zeitgeist for fashions in language and subject matter. What words are emerging or fading in society?

— Map associations: Handwrite your subject on blank paper. Draw a circle around it. Extend spokes to other circles and fill in related topics. Where are the gaps? The connections? The distinctions?

— Stockpile keywords: Make a laundry list of keywords related to your message. Reflect on their nuances of meaning. Which ones appeal? Which ones will be useful?

— Mine the mother lode: List related words from a thesaurus. Even if you don't use them, you mentally plant seeds that can sprout later in useful phrasings.

— Inventory quotations: Research pithy sayings related to your message. Absorb their novelty in expression. Can you play off them?

Now take a stab at your message: Let's say you start with something basic. For example, say you're a management expert, and you're writing about loyalty. You decide you want to take a bit of a contrarian view, so you pen, "Loyalty makes people do bad things." Hmm, okay, you have a general message. Good start.

Now start refining it with some circling. Consider various meanings of the concept, map elements of management affected by it, list a few keywords, copy a few quotations. Now you might redraft to be more specific: "Loyalty subverts good decision making."

That's progress. Your language is more precise, your focus narrower. You probably don't feel like you've hit the bull's-eye, but you have a better fix on your aspirations. You have shown, and documented, wide-ranging and thorough thinking, perhaps benefiting from a mix of daydreaming, analysis, and synthesis.

Amending

When you're done with circling, your mind has toured a big neighborhood. You've run down some blind alleys. You've peered in a lot of windows and down a few bulkheads. Sorting through what you've seen, you've settled on an approach—a message—that best fits your tastes.

But you know the one you've chosen still isn't perfect. If nothing else, your message lacks novelty. Try as you may, you slip into clichés. You may even realize that you have circled right back to the beginning, to the obvious. Geez! you exclaim.

This may not happen to you. But you're in good company if it does. And it's not necessarily a bad thing. Great books appear all the time that restate ageless wisdom. If you find yourself in this situation, you may be receiving a signal that you are ready to extend or enhance an old idea. You have a fresh envelope for an old message.

Whatever your message, it's time to refine it. Here are some aids for amending:

— Express it with metaphor: In his essay, "Politics and the English Language," George Orwell advised writers to look from the start for a way to express an idea with an image or idiom. Can you find a sturdy metaphorical vehicle to carry your thoughts?

— Draw new distinctions: Clear thinking depends on distinguishing between one thing and something quite similar. People often conflate two, three, or more similar concepts. Can you tease yours apart and delineate nuances?

— Start journaling: Writing spurs thinking, so while cooking up your main message, play around with related ideas. Record your musings, brainstorms, questions, and ideas. Write fast, don't stop, don't delete.

— Personalize and humanize: State your message in the way you would to a loved one. Why should people you know intimately care?

— Float your idea: At every chance, try your message on friends. Don't tell them they're test subjects. See at the next barbecue which words evoke the reaction you seek.

Now take another stab at your message. Let's assume you're still working on loyalty. You've done some journaling, pondered distinctions, tried variations out on a few friends. You draft an update: "Loyalty poisons ethical decision making."

Okay, you've narrowed your focus again, and you've drawn a key distinction about the kind of decision making you're talking about. You've also chosen "poison" as a metaphorical way to express treachery, confusion, dysfunction, even lethality. You could try to go farther, but this is terrific progress.

Don't worry that your change in wording may be small; the tiniest change in an umbrella message can represent a huge turn in the treatment of your book. Making the right turn can make all the difference in driving toward your destination.

Don't erase obsolete thoughts from your pencil work. You may consider some of your expressions to be platitudes, worn-out metaphors, stale idioms, inaccurate distinctions, but if they marched across your mind once, they probably had a reason. Let them take up permanent residence. You may find them helpful tomorrow.

Firming

Up to now, you've worked mostly by hand. Your notes are probably a mess. Arrows, circles, asterisks, cross outs, highlighting—a clutter spreads across your tablet like the flotsam on a teenager's bedroom floor. But that's okay, because you haven't gotten overly attached to your ideas. In fact, you're dying to clean them up.

To finish this step in the Stairway to Earth process, abandon pencil and paper. Go to your keyboard and create two documents. This marks the beginning of your electronic paper trail, a trail of deliverables that will lead, eventually, to that winning manuscript:

MESSAGE STATEMENT

TITLE BRAINSTORMING

For the message statement, open a new document and draft the point of your book. Keep it to one sentence. If you've done your work up to now, you already have a serviceable message on your tablet. It may not be great, but it will be good. As you type it, try to go one better. Use potent nouns and verbs.

You may question why it's so important to wait until now to go to the keyboard. Isn't waiting a matter of preference? Maybe, but my experience is that composing on a keyboard puts your mind in a different place. You pass from the playground of possibilities to the lobby of professional practice. You are no longer just fooling around.

If you're still working on that loyalty message, what might go on here? Maybe your friends asked at the barbecue for an example to illustrate your point (they always do). At first, you couldn't seem to fire them up with your message. So you ratcheted it up. You said, "Loyalty poisons ethical decision making in Washington, D.C." Ooh boy, that got their attention.

And that was a good feeling. Your politico friends were riveted, and you had a core audience. But then a book about Washington politics is not quite what you had in mind. You're a management expert, not a political scientist. So you want to firm your message in another way. Maybe you need to relate it better to corporate life. How about: "Loyalty poisons ethical decision making in hiring, firing, and promotions."

After drafting the message, open another new document. This one is for brainstorming titles. Type in all the titles you can think of. Many will come from your pencil notes. Again, be sure to keep everything you write down. Not only might you like something tomorrow that you didn't like today, new patterns will emerge from old streams of thinking.

Throughout the first step in the Stairway to Earth process, you may feel you're going to way too much effort to accomplish a simple task. Truth be known, the task is far less simple— or easy—than it appears. The mind is a pretty big playground. You've got to get all the children in your head under control and walking in step.

Remarkably, message development often takes days—a chunk of hours spent here, a chunk there, some deep thinking in the shower, and a long talk with a friend or two. To increase your effectiveness, keep some added rules of thumb in mind:

— Search for the box: Though many people praise "out-of-the-box" thinking during the creative process, remember that, to define your message, you eventually need to define the box. What's in? What's out?

— Capture everything: Essayist E. B. White suggested in his classic, *The Elements of Style,* that writers had to take "occasional wing shots" for "bringing down the bird of thought as it flashes by." In other words, don't let good game get away. Keep a pencil at hand to skewer good ideas as they pop in front of you.

— Engage intellect *and* emotion: Humanizing a message engages a reader's feelings. Drawn by the heartstrings as well as by curiosity, readers lean close to hear your story.

— Develop your message on two levels: Explicitly address your concrete topic. Implicitly, if only via inference, address life. A book about loyalty in business can teach a lot about loyalty in life.

— Prize simplicity: In the same way that powerful designs (think iPod) package complex technology in simple products, powerful insights package complex ideas in simple words.

— Put accuracy first: Create a message that's clear before getting caught up in creating one that's catchy. Give preference to saying the right thing. Then figure out how to say it in the right way.

— Count on the unconscious: Your mind does an awful lot of work while you're asleep, mowing the lawn, and slouching at the beach. Don't bear down too hard. Your neurons, given a little R&R, will reward you.

If all goes well, you will find just the right message early on—and of course the right title. But set your expectations appropriately: Don't count on ringing the bell of perfection at the start. Instead, consider your message and title works in progress. You'll have plenty of chances to tune them later.

When I started this book, I knew I wanted to write about "How to Write a Serious Book." I tried to come up with catchy titles: "Getting with the Program," "Write Right," "Think Write," "The Missing Link in Book Writing," "Overcoming Writing Vertigo." But I also wanted to follow Orwell's advice, capturing my idea in metaphor. Could I somehow come up with an image to reflect the stepwise nature of the process?

In my head, I had this picture of the main problem: a writer struggling in a netherworld of confused ideas, looking for a systematic path to developing a clear argument. "Stairway to Heaven" occurred to me as representing a magical yet stepwise way of transporting the writer to clarity. (Clichés always seem to pop to mind first.) But then it hit me: Just the opposite fit much better: "Stairway to Earth."

Bear in mind that you will iterate you message all the way through the completion of your manuscript. You shouldn't feel that you have to "finish" on this first step. Although I came up with the Stairway title before writing, I usually don't find a title nearly so early. It is enough to brainstorm, rework prototype language, and rethink insights. The point is to come up with something good that you can move ahead with.

You will never stop wishing you could develop a message with the same speed as a star musician develops a melody. Who doesn't wish he or she was like, say, George Harrison, for whom "Here Comes the Sun" poured out all at once at sunrise at Eric Clapton's house? (And that wasn't the only time that happened.)

But this wish is unrealistic.

The good news is that even if you're not a natural, you can employ a logical process to mature your ideas. It does take time. Days may stretch to weeks. But that's not such a bad thing. The hunt for a simple truth in the beginning can be the most thrilling part of writing a book. Take time to savor the chase.

The message you come up with is more valuable than it looks. You may think, Hey, it's just one sentence. But that one sentence gives you an unadorned statement of direction to guide your journey. It will serve as your refrain—your personal "Here Comes the Sun"—as you take the next step on the Stairway to Earth, Step 2: Right Argument.

YOUR PAPER TRAIL

STEP 1

✓ MESSAGE STATEMENT

✓ TITLE INVENTORY

CHAPTER 2

RIGHT ARGUMENT

Many years ago, I worked on a book with three people from the management-consulting firm now called Accenture. We met in Boston to talk about the sequence of chapters. Studying the draft table of contents, one of the consultants looked up and said to his coauthors, "But is this 'meesee'?"

I stared from my side of the table and thought, "Huh?"

"Meesee" was actually MECE, I soon learned—"mutually exclusive and collectively exhaustive." The consultants felt that testing an argument for whether it was MECE was an important step in analyzing the rigor of their thinking. When the consultant posed this question, he was essentially asking: Have we broken the puzzle of the problem into distinct pieces, included everything necessary, with nothing overlapping?

I mention this meeting because these consultants were onto something when it came to books. In building the flow of concept and content, authors often repeat in later chapters the points stated in earlier ones. (This is a more common error than you think.) Saying again in chapter 2 or chapter 3 what you said in chapter 1 is failing to follow the ME in MECE. Not good.

Think back to my song-writing analogy. Repeating a song's refrain is fine. Repeating its verses isn't. The first is a pleasant echo. The other is redundancy. What goes in verse 2 (or chapter 2) should dovetail with verse 1, not repeat it.

You'll see soon how MECE fits into this chapter. But let's back up for a moment. When you finished the last chapter, you had crystallized your message in a phrase and short title. That was the first step in figuring out "what the book says." Now you want to expand what the message says, but do so in a controlled way.

Here are three tasks I recommend in this second step on the Stairway to Earth:

MARKET THE MESSAGE

ARGUE WITH RIGOR

DOCUMENT THE ESSENCE

Market the message

If someone heard about your message and title, and they said, "Tell me more!" what would you say? Where would you start? Imagine you are producing a trailer for a full-length movie. What items would you put in the script, in what order?

Another good way to organize your thinking is to think about the job as preparing to write a marketing brochure. The simple formula followed by marketing writers is problem-solution-features-benefits. You have a product, a book. What would you say for each of these four categories?

Take your pencil again and play around with some words for each marketing-brochure category. Goal number one: Find words that are "right"—that is, accurate. Above all, you want to express *exactly* what your book has to offer. Don't worry if your words are not catchy. Try to get your compass bearing within a few degrees of true north.

Come up with a half dozen thoughts for each category. Try to express the questions your book answers with fresh and timely language. If your message was the umbrella phrase, what comes under it? Don't think of this task as creating text for the book. That puts too much pressure on you, probably dulling your brainstorming.

Depending on your book, you should adjust the categories. I often change the problem-solution-features-benefits formula to problem-solution-presentation-promise. After describing the problem (or issue) and big-picture solution, I present the sequence of my argument. As an alternative, you might try another formula: issue-resolution-steps-results. This might work well with a policy book. Or for a history book focused on events you could try subject-chronology-climax-meaning. Or character-complication-development-climax for a narrative focused on one or several people. Or problem-solution-steps-benefits with a how-to or self-help book.

Here are aids for fleshing out the message:

— Parse the subject or problem: List top-of-mind components of the subject you address. Identify the items that produce acute curiosity or pain for your core readers.

— Parse the outcome or solution: List top-of-mind components of the results you will cover. Don't be exhaustive. Cite the items of greatest priority.

— List edgy stuff: Note concepts or content that will prick your readers' attention. What would wake up even your neighbor who doesn't give a hoot about your interests?

— List the sweet stuff: What "mind candy" do you have? Choose the most mouth-watering material.

— Push your metaphor: If you have a metaphor to carry your initial message, check whether it can carry the whole book. Malcolm Gladwell's "tipping point" is an example.

— Anticipate the elevator: Imagine giving the venerable "elevator pitch" to an editor. What words would you choose to sell the need, solution, and promise of the book?

— Lean on friends (again): Talk to those friends at the barbecue. How do they respond? A caution: Don't overweight comments from people who don't represent your core audience.

As in the last chapter, circle the stuff you like best. Reflect on it. At this stage in the book-writing process, you're still a gardener in early season. Water, fertilize, weed, nurture. Count on the light of your mind, with a little time, to turn crude sprouts into a mature harvest.

It's not too early to think about some practical concerns that will come up later: Can you support your blossoming message with good content? Is the research required by your direction feasible? And how fertile is the market for this idea?

Argue with rigor

A successful trade book moves the reader along a trajectory of increasing insight. If the book starts at point A, readers will expect it to ascend to points B, C, D, and thence at least to G or H. At H, they expect to arrive at the top of some inspiring climb. They want to declare, "Nice view!"

Now is the time to think about the route of that climb. In recent years, the Internet has encouraged reading and writing in a web-like, hyperlinked way. This is good in many ways. And you may want to think about hyperlinks if you're doing an e-book. But a print book demands a linear approach. Whatever else you do, you must guide readers through a progression. Readers will expect it, in fact will thirst for it.

If a print book has any characteristic the Internet cannot rival, it is the power of progression. Use it to your advantage. It represents a big part of the value you bring to book-length writing as an author. To be sure, some books don't demand a progression—guidebooks, textbooks, manuals, travelogues. Still, they may well be better for it, giving increasing insight along with a growing compendium of information.

You can also think of your book in chunks. What chunk comes first, second, and so on? Or you can think of it as a puzzle. How do the pieces fit? Just make sure your conceptualization is something the reader can follow—make sure it provides a clear, orderly, reasoned, and pleasing progression in the writing. The reader must be able to easily connect the dots and, in turn, feel transported to ever higher levels of insight.

I'm a believer that every book has a natural organization. Your job is simply to find it. As a starting point, try sequencing according to chronology. Or by developmental steps. Or the evolution of an idea. Or level of priority. Or phases of personal growth. Or by geography. You may not find the principles emerging at first that clearly govern your organization. But if nothing else, simple trial and error can sometimes show the way.

The organization you choose should carry the reader on a smooth journey. This doesn't mean that the progression moves steadily forward. It may go to the side, or even loop back—digressions work well for context, background, and side stories. What it does mean is that it works to provide one grand tableau, in which the reader sees easily how everything fits together, and fits together in the order in which you've presented it.

Pablo Picasso, in his early years, drew many pictures of a favorite topic in his native Spain: bullfighters. In many of his works, he captured the essence of a man with cape in just eight or ten strokes. If ever there was inspiration in art for clean thinking in an argument, it was Picasso: Capture the essence of your book in eight to ten lines that create a delightful whole.

Here are some aids for coming up with your argument:

— Plan a quest: All books serve to guide readers on a quest for more learning. Ask yourself: What is the "plot" for my quest? What are the episodes?

— Build pyramids: Build your case one block at a time. What goes at the bottom? At the top? The classic negotiator's bible, *Getting to Yes,* is an example.

— Fill frameworks: Do you like to capture thoughts with geometric shapes? Diamonds or squares or circles? Check how Stephen Covey uses a double pyramid to organize his thoughts in *The Seven Habits of Highly Effective People.*

— Extend metaphors: Take your title metaphor a step further, using it to structure your argument. Thomas L. Friedman's *The World is Flat* is an example. So is *Stairway to Earth.*

— Reverse directions: Test unconventional patterns. Work from effect to cause. Try packaging your idea with an upbeat approach—or a downbeat one (do you write your investment book as *The Coming Crash* or *Make a*

Million in the Bubble?)

— Compose cliffhangers: What will draw the reader from the end of one chapter to the next? What are your segues?

— Road-test logic: Talk through your progression. Recite it out loud to yourself. Explain it to others. Where does it break down?

Enthusiasts of many kinds often refer to the "pretty lines" of their subject. Rock climbers talk about pretty lines on cliffs. Car lovers talk about pretty lines on car bodies. Spelunkers talk about them in caves. The line of your book may not jump out at first. But like a climber or an artist or a designer, you should work to find the pretty line.

And don't be shy about copying. If another book uses a useful device to structure its argument, by all means think about borrowing the approach. Say you want to write a book about chair design. No reason not to look at other books on design and mimic a winning pattern. Don't worry about being called a copycat. Your execution of the manuscript will be utterly unique.

Document the essence

If you've stuck with a pencil so far, you have another mess on your hands—probably a couple of tablets' worth. Now is the time to finish this step on the Stairway to Earth. Adding to the paper trail you started in chapter one, create two new documents at your keyboard:

Book précis

Table of contents

What is a précis? At its simplest, it is a summary. I prefer the term précis to refer to this all-critical document, because a lot of people think of summaries as imprecise and dull. Précis echoes the roots of the French verb *"préciser,"* to "specify." It suggests precision. Précis strikes me as the right word to describe the job of making your argument.

In academia, "précis" also means a precise replica—in miniature—of the logic, information, and emphasis of an original work. That pretty much describes what you want to write at the moment. But unlike many academic précis, try to stay under three hundred words, one page. Imagine your finished book and reproduce a thumbnail.

While you create a précis, also create a table of contents. Draft six to twelve chapter titles. Choose words that show the progression of your argument. Add descriptive subtitles if needed. Be brief. Don't exceed one line per chapter title. You want the table of contents to reflect just the ribcage of your thinking, so you can identify misplaced parts.

Remember not to forget what you learned in the last chapter: drawing distinctions, defining your box, engaging mind and emotion, making your message work on two levels. Use any of these techniques to enhance the clarity of your thinking.

Here are some other tips I favor:

— Seek elegance: If you're an engineer, high praise is to be told your design is "elegant"— ingeniously simple, free of extra parts, able to do the job completely. Good advice for a writer.

— Remember MECE: "Mutually exclusive and collectively exhaustive"—a nice principle for sharpening thought. It helps with elegance, and in locating that "pretty line."

— Ascend ladders: Readers expect to learn as they read. Make sure your argument goes up the ladder of insight. Four to eight rungs are plenty.

— Deliver closure: Every book evokes new questions along the way. If your argument has begged a question, you should answer it. Don't leave people hanging.

— Beware fallacies: Your reader will go much harder on your logic than you will. Root out misleading analogies, sweeping generalizations, false dilemmas, and loaded language.

— Call for action: At the end of the book, readers will look for an inspiring send-off. What can you give them to propel them beyond the covers of the book?

— Think digital: The future belongs to e-books. Media companies now cut books into pieces and sell them in chunks. Keep the salability of chunks in mind.

Now that you've written a précis and table of contents, look back at your message and title from the last chapter. How do they look? A little askew? Iterate them if they don't hold up to your new thinking.

Don't worry at this point if you don't produce a catchy précis and table of contents. And resist being tempted into endless wordsmithing to find something elegant, because you will lose freshness. Remember that you've already started to get overly familiar with your ideas. You need to conserve perspective to judge them. For now, make your best shot and set it aside.

And by the way, save your old drafts. Sometimes you'll decide to go back to them. More than once I have realized in the morning that, deafened by the din of my work the day before, I threw out the best recording of my inner music. Then I'm glad to have kept the oldies but goodies still lying around. Remarkably, a few times, I have even thrown out a third draft and gone back to the first.

When you finish this step, you will have a full, even if still skeletal, vision of your book. This is a landmark in your book development. From here on, you will expand and refine continuously. That's next, in Stairway to Earth, Step 3: Right Differentiation.

YOUR PAPER TRAIL

STEP 2

✓ BOOK PRÉCIS

✓ TABLE OF CONTENTS

CHAPTER 3

RIGHT DIFFERENTIATION

I was once advising a first-time author about a book on leadership. She was several months into her research, and she had interviewed a dozen luminary leaders. She had also recently dined with a powerful business-conference impresario. Having told him about her book, she was dazed by his response: He said she had *absolutely nothing new to say.*

After all her work—nothing new to say? Could it be true?

I actually found this unlikely. After all, the author had picked the brains of the smartest people around. She had worked under the tutelage of leadership role models from industry and government around the world. My guess is that the impresario was essentially challenging her—in the way all writers must challenge themselves: To figure out what's new about a book's message and argument.

The reality is that little is altogether new about many topics. Leadership, love, sex, strategy, painting, policy, pottery, dieting, you name it. Smart people over the millennia have wrestled with the eternal truths of work and life. They have been writing about them since the advent of the stone tablet. The question is: What sets your book apart?

So crucial is answering this question that you should make it a discrete step in the book-development process. What fresh approach are you bringing to your topic? How are you going to make your book sing to readers in a new way? Answer this question explicitly, not just because you need to set your book apart. Answer it because it will help you hone your argument to a sharper point.

If you're quick, lucky, and smart enough, maybe you're writing about something that has emerged for the first time. Good for you. But more often, existing coverage of people, things, stories, and ideas overlaps yours. And it's up to you to find—or open up—an underserved slot on a bookstore (or online store) shelf.

One thing always works in your favor: Your combination of background, education, experience, and temperament are unique. So are your relationships, worldview, and style. If you simply let your book reflect you, you'll automatically have a somewhat different approach. Sometimes that is all you need.

Still, you'll normally have to deliver more. In the first place, you'll want to make a contribution that's new in a way that goes beyond what your personal touch brings to it. You'll want to make a difference. Who wants to write a me-too book?

In the second place, you have to stand out in a pretty big crowd. After all, you must catch the attention of an agent, publishers, and readers who are overloaded with great reading. According to industry authority R. R. Bowker, a remarkable 290,000 books were published in the U.S. in 2010 alone. Think about that for a moment. That's about three times the number of items sold in a Wal-Mart super-store.

Every book category bursts with titles. No matter what you write, other authors can outgun you by virtue of sheer volume. Consider 2009. The number of books published in the U.S. in science alone was 13,555; in education, 9,510; in business 8,838; in sociology/economics, 24,423. How is your book going to appeal to people with so many others shouting at the same time?

In the third place, you'll want to attempt to one-up other authors. Ever notice how, if you're golfing alone (or skiing or shooting baskets), you can hit some lousy drives (or turns or shots)—and who cares? If you're with others, you raise your game a notch. And if you're with people much better than you, *they* can raise you a notch.

Be grateful if your competitors set the standard high. In the same way as an athlete does, you can use the excellence of others to give you a kick in the backside—and inspire you—to put a spin and finish on your book so it shines in a new way.

I recommend three tasks to differentiate your message and argument in this third step on the Stairway to Earth:

STUDY YOUR RIVALS

FIND YOUR DIFFERENCE

CAPTURE THE GIST

Study your rivals

If you're in a hurry to get your book written, you may not like this advice: Slow down. Get some books like yours. Read them and take notes. Reflect. Get more books. Read. Repeat. If you like to devour books, you'll enjoy this step, sampling a buffet you've probably eyed hungrily for a long time.

But don't devour just for pleasure. Read like a writer. Look at how existing books divvy up and address the category in which you plan to write. Study titles, subtitles, tables of contents. Dissect introductions, chapter openings, and closing chapters. Authors often signal their intent right at the start, and you can compare and contrast your vision with theirs.

Pretty simple, really. You have to think of yourself as an entrepreneur. Say, as a sideline, you planned to open an Italian restaurant in a city that already had five others. What would you do? You would survey the competition to get a feel for various approaches and locations. You would eat at the restaurants to study décor, menu, pricing, and service. You would note which ones get the most traffic by counting filled tables and cars in the parking lot.

Same for books. Note what others offer, and note what you can do better. What can you cook up to add to the book's interior? How can you serve customers in a more intriguing way? How can you tap your readers' needs and wants—as determined by their age, affluence, ethnicity, gender, education, profession, whatever.

Don't worry if your audience is the same as that of your competitors. Although you don't want to market the same book to the same audience, you do want to market your book to proven book-buying readers. If you're opening an

Italian restaurant, the more Italian-food lovers in your market the better—so long as they like to eat Italian regularly.

Here are ways to study rivals:

— Browse bookstores: Go to both chain stores and independents. Study especially the titles stocked in multiple copies. These are the books the stores' buyers expect to sell briskly—and will in turn pose the most competition. (Browsing library shelves is not a substitute. Few aging titles will compete with yours.)

— Browse books online: Visit an online bookseller and browse via keywords. Sort titles by bestsellers and by publication date. Click links to books with similar ideas to yours.

— Browse categories online: Go online and browse by category. Look at books that are likely to be shelved with yours. In your niche, what books are your rivals?

— Get sales figures: Check sales rankings on amazon.com and bn.com. Visit titlez.com to compare sales. If you have access via an agent, get actual nationwide checkout-counter figures from Nielsen BookScan.

— Poll colleagues: Ask people with your interest what books they admire. What do they dislike? Why?

— Collect reviews: Book reviewers often cite books' differentiating features. Read both published reviews and postings online to glean opportunities.

While you're at it, remember that many breakthrough ideas—in books and life—come from putting together unlike ingredients. Spend time looking at book structures, arguments, and treatments, in fields and genres completely unlike yours. As a mental exercise, imagine mimicking their styles.

Find your difference

Now decide what you've learned. Invariably, you will decide to make a few mid-course corrections in your message or argument. Then again, you may decide to turn your argument in an entirely new direction. If you stay on top of your professional game, you probably won't get caught making a 90 – or 180-degree turn—in effect throwing out your initial idea. But if you do, now is the time.

Plan in any case for a burst of creative thinking of a different kind. You will be asking, How will I "sell" my idea to readers? From the perspective of a salesperson, consider what spurs your customers to buy. Bring your idea at least one evolutionary step beyond where you imagined.

Your book is a "product," and getting a product to sell calls for more than manufacturing. You have to think about marketing. Although a book isn't a tube of toothpaste, imagine you have to sell it like one. This is a useful exercise, by the way, for more than idea development. It will serve you later when you propose how to partner with your publisher to sell the finished product.

One device for guiding your thinking is a business-school favorite called the 4 Ps of marketing. The Ps, developed by professors at Harvard Business School, stand for the four parts of a marketing plan: product, promotion, placement, and price. Though developed for things like toothpaste and pet food, they apply just as well to books.

You already have a good start on the first of the 4 Ps, product. In studying competitive books, you can't help but ask, How does my product distinguish itself in terms of concept, argument, structure, content, and treatment?

Now start thinking about the next three Ps: As for promotion, ask, How do other authors promote their books uniquely and powerfully? Promotion alone can differentiate many books. Ask yourself how it will figure into yours.

As for placement, publishers will distribute your book to stores, online, and in special bulk orders. Do you have any ideas for other sales channels? Some books never ship to booksellers. They go through gift shops, workshops, corporate pep-talk events, business conferences, and direct sales through the Internet.

As for price, your publisher will set the dollar amount, in part to appeal to your core readers. At this point in your book's development, you might want to substitute "value added" for price. What value are you offering that others do not offer that you can ask readers to pay for?

Something else to think about at this point: Bookstores will shelve (and promote) your book by category, and you want it shelved so your readers find it. Say you write a book about Henry David Thoreau's bean garden. You write about hoeing beans, but what you're really talking about is Thoreau's view of life. If you leave the category unclear, bookstores may shelve it under Gardening instead of Nature or Philosophy.

So clarify your positioning so you won't get mis-shelved—and never sell a copy. Also position your book in the category popular with your core audience. I was once in a book-marketing meeting with a business-book editor. Her publishing house had come out with a health-care reform book by a business-strategy consultant. The book-marketing folks had debated whether to position the book for the author's core audience – managers – or for health-care professionals. What would work best?

Once the books started selling, the marketers got their answer fast. Books sold from the management shelf in stores outsold those shelved in health care by *ten times*. The lesson: Keep your authorial eye on your core audience. Beware trying to be everything to everybody. If your book has crossover potential, promote it in related categories after the book is published. From the start, decide on your target and position your firepower in that direction.

Here are ways to find your difference:

— Draw some differentiating lines: As you find differences, list distinctions in black and white. A good technique: List what your book is *not* (this book is not a health-care book, not a gardening book, and so on).

— Clarify your authority: What is your signature expertise and experience? In what pond are you the big fish? In what niche are you the master?

— Reconsider trends: Most books, from idea to print, take at least two years to finish. Describe the market into which your book will launch while anticipating its evolution two to three years out.

— Clarify your levels: If on the surface you cover the same message as another book, what is the message or theme you drive at underneath? Describe your surface argument and the way you will draw from it greater meaning.

— Trumpet your platform: Your publisher will want you to help sell books. What marketing and sales channels can you tap? Do you give keynote speeches? Run workshops? Sell books in bulk through your company?

When David Nichol and I wrote *The One-Minute Meditator,* we answered just these questions. For example: We explicitly decided what our book was not— not a spiritual book, not a religious one, not a manual of fringe practices. We clarified our authority as based on Dr. Nichol's training, clinical practice, and long experience. We anticipated the book would enter the market at a promising time—just as health-care providers began to offer meditation as a mainstream stress treatment. And we trumpeted our platform, which was built on the demonstrated interest of health-care giants in selling our book in bulk, not just through bookstores.

Each of these decisions influenced how we tailored the message, structured the argument, and wrote the book. We didn't let marketing concerns consume us during book development. On the other hand, we knew that few books survive long without a solid plan for reaching readers. People today have so many choices, and you have to figure out how your book will be their book of choice.

Clear distinctions, captured in an interesting way, can make all the difference. Consider the book *Men Are from Mars, Women Are from Venus.* The title says it all: The sexes come from two different planets, and the book will tell you how.

Capture the gist

To finish this step on the Stairway to Earth, commit your research and thinking to two documents.

COMPETING BOOKS LOG

POSITIONING JOURNAL

For your competing books log, enter notes from your study of rivals. An easy way to do this is to find the books online and cut/paste their details into your document: title, subtitle, author, publisher, date, sales rank, cover image, summary excerpts and book-review excerpts. Add notes about book structure, table of contents, weaknesses, and untapped market niches.

Add to these notes your research from bookstore trips. Expect to refer often to this document—as you keep working on differentiation, refining your argument, writing your manuscript, and shaping your marketing plan. The more you learn about your competition, the more clearly you will see your book's unique direction.

For your positioning journal, go to your computer and pour out your thoughts. The journal is not a document for publication but instead a log of reflections. Describe your market position. Be especially thoughtful in answering questions about authority and platform—key concerns of publishers.

One positioning trick authors use is to compare their book with a classic that still sells well. If you can, find a perennial favorite that uses a structure or treatment like yours. You'll find that you can sometimes spark a remarkably vivid picture of your intentions with a comparison. This is something akin to describing people by comparing them to someone else— "My brother looks just like Tom Cruise with blonde hair."

Consider some book proposals bought by publishers: A book on current affairs was pitched as "a *Freakonomics*-style guide to the mechanics of electoral politics." Another book, on the effect of sky-high gasoline costs, was called a "thought experiment on the same scale as *The World Without Us*." A third, a humor book, was pitched as "*Marley & Me* with parrots."

Don't give short shrift to work on your competing-books and positioning documents. If you brainstorm much at all, the documents should run to many pages—if for no reason other than the fun in exploring possibilities. The ultimate goal isn't creativity, though. It is clarity. Nail down your positioning coordinates exactly.

Now go back one step and recast your table of contents to match. You want to iterate your argument to get it just right. In the next step on the Stairway to Earth—Right Content—you rely on the argument for your marching orders. So stay with your work on differentiation until you feel you can tick off your book's distinguishing features like the items on a laundry list. If you do, no impresario will ever accuse you of having absolutely nothing new to say.

YOUR PAPER TRAIL

STEP 3

✓COMPETING BOOKS LOG

✓POSITIONING JOURNAL

CHAPTER 4

RIGHT CONTENT

At an orientation for first-year college students, a lanky, graying professor stood at the podium giving advice. An audience of incoming students, my son one of them, sat with the tuition-paying parents. It was Sunday morning, but the professor seemed to know how to keep people awake. To a crowd of boomers about to part with their children, he read a poem by Billy Collins about how you can never repay your mother. It was a big hit.

As the professor flipped through his remarks, Post-it notes and taped-on addendums fluttered from his pages. He stopped speaking off and on to untangle them. Though a caricature of the disheveled professor, he and his behavior began to have a kind of academic charm, and I sensed the fluttering pieces contained all the good stuff he had to say.

The professor eventually came to the subject of writing, and he made a point that, for me, reverberated like no other: The college would teach first-year students how to provide *evidence* for their opinions.

Now there was a timeless message, I thought. How many times while writing, had I unexpectedly come up empty on evidence for what I wanted to say? Not one shred of evidence did I have. No data. No expert testimony. No literature support. No case study. No first-hand accounts. No juicy quotes. Not even a breezy anecdote.

Authors often come to me in roughly this state. They have a terrific concept but not much material to demonstrate what they have to say. It's almost as if they think a strong enough concept can float a reader over a shallow pool of content. Passion for a subject has that effect: You get so enamored with what you have to say that you almost forget you have to have evidence to convince your reader.

The story of the professor offers a friendly reminder: Authors should take the time to check that they have plenty of the two C's of writing: concept *and* content. "Concept" includes ideas, messages, insights, and conclusions. "Content" includes research data, study results, anecdotes, case stories, expert testimony, interview transcripts, narrative scenes, and so on. Concept is assertion. Content is evidence. You need plenty of both.

Watching the professor, I imagined that his main remarks, on regular-size sheets of paper, contained the core of his argument. The flaps of paper were the evidence. I began to wonder what gems were on those itinerant slips that seemed to get away from him. In any case, he gave a graphic illustration of how you need lots of evidence to keep an audience awake.

The last three chapters focused mostly on concept, that is, on the conceptual skeleton that forms the structure of your book. Now is the time to focus on the content, or evidence, that puts flesh on the skeletal bones. For this step on the Stairway to Earth, I advise three tasks:

INVENTORY CONTENT

BRIDGE THE CHASMS

BUILD A WAREHOUSE

Inventory content

Another way of thinking of concept is as a train. Content is then the freight the train carries. You wouldn't think of running a railroad with unfilled train cars. The same for writing a book. You don't want concept rolling down the tracks on its own. There would be too much noise, too little delivered.

So in this phase of the book-writing process, I suggest you inventory your existing content for every chapter in your book. It is easy to *think* there is enough content and then later find there is far more chaff than wheat. So be systematic and ask: Do I have enough material to load each concept car with concrete evidence.

You don't have to go into too much detail in this job, at least not yet. List your chapters down the left side of a tablet. On the right, note chunks of content that will go in each. If some content works for two or more chapters, allocate it to the chapter that suits it best.

The content will depend on the kind of book you are writing. In some books, you may want anecdotes, case histories, and first-hand interviews. In others, only hard data can carry your argument. If you're writing a book about sleep deprivation, and you require peer-reviewed research, be sure you have access to the right studies. Also be sure you have enough to spread more than a veneer of it across your chapters.

The same goes for books with a narrative component. If you need narratives to show an historical event, be sure you can obtain enough interviews or other first-hand accounts to serve as verifiable evidence. If key characters won't give you access, you may face a showstopper.

Don't go to the trouble (yet) of doing the actual research where you have gaps. Simply confirm, to your satisfaction, that you can obtain what you need. If you need hard data, scan the literature to be sure the data exist. If you need narrative scenes, verify that the documents, media, and people who can supply them are actually available.

I once proposed to do a narrative book on a big brand-name consumer-goods company. I aimed to portray its work as a role model. I assumed early on that I could get access to company managers. The publicity chief encouraged me in this regard. Lo and behold, after a year, I was shut out when the company decided to stay closemouthed. I lost a lot of work and time.

So be realistic in your assessment of content availability. Also be realistic about quality. Not only should material strongly support your argument, it should be original. And if the content isn't new, you should be planning to use it in a new way. If you're writing about leadership, for example, material on South Pole explorer Ernest Shackleton isn't new. A lot of people know the story of his journey to save his crew after his ship was crushed in the Antarctic ice.

In any case, be careful not to retread material in familiar ways—unless you're certain the market has room for two books on the same subject, using the same material. Remember, too, that most readers demand variety. In most cases, you cannot sustain a book-length work solely with academic research data, or breezy anecdotes, or personal experience, or quotes from interviews. You need a mix. Even memoirs benefit from source material beyond what resides in the author's memory.

Also beware of overexposure. If you plan to use a great story in chapter 2 to make one point in your argument, you cannot usually come back to it in any significant way later, unless you make new points with added detail. Most material, asked to run a second lap in your book, can look awfully tired.

Bridge the chasms

As you inventory your content, look for sources of material to fill any information gaps you may have. In almost every book, you will discover that your argument carries you onto terrain where you have almost no content on hand. This invariably stems from your asking yourself some entirely new questions—and you'll have to find new material to support your answers.

As an example, in *Wal-Smart,* a book on how to compete with Wal-Mart, author Bill Marquard argued that companies could outcompete the big retailer in many ways. The retailer isn't good at everything, after all. One way to stand out in shoppers' minds is to practice greater social responsibility. This message was the logical extension of Marquard's argument that all kinds of retailers could find ways to compete in the Wal-Mart economy.

But it wasn't until Marquard fleshed out his argument—and differentiated it from other books—that he realized he needed fresh content for this section of his book. His earlier chapters had focused on other aspects of competing with the giant. So he had to ask: Can I get the material I need? It turned out the research trove was deep. It informed and enriched the last chapter in his book—and incidentally opened a new chapter in his consulting business.

Like Marquard, you have to think through the content you'll need. Make some phone calls, poke around on the web, do a literature search. See if your research plan is feasible. Sometimes you will stumble into a content void. That's when you have to rethink. Maybe you have to iterate your concept again. Maybe you have to drop a chapter, or merge a couple of them. Usually you can reconfigure your book to sidestep an issue you can't support.

Build a warehouse

In this fourth step on the Stairway to Earth, you should at least informally weigh your material for adequacy. Scan what you have and decide "by feel" if you have enough. And if you're still serious about writing the book, start to build a formal structure for your research library. Here are the two items I recommend adding to the paper trail that will lead to your manuscript:

DIGITAL REFERENCE FILES

PAPER REFERENCE FILES

If you're passionate about your subject, you can easily delve into research without a thought about how to organize what you find. You poke around the web, crack several books, mark up a dozen articles. Soon, a stack of marked-up paper rises on your desk. The stack multiplies into several. Before you know it, your several piles slide into one, and you can't find anything. It can be maddening.

You have a material-handling problem. To avoid it, think early about how to organize a warehouse worth of material—because that's how much you need for a book. In effect, you will need an inventory system to catalogue and retrieve all the material you sock away. If possible, the system should be electronic. Even if you write from paper notes, scan originals into your computer so you can find them with a keystroke.

Special software makes this easy. I'll explain more in chapter 10. For now, create at least one computer folder for your research. Dump into it all notes, articles, excerpts, web pages, and other material. So long as everything includes keywords related to your book argument, you can find what you need with a simple computer search. You don't want your research warehouse to be like the boxes in your grandparents' attic—full of heirlooms and memorabilia—none of which you can put your hands on when you need them.

Next, create a manila folder for each chapter in your book. Even in the electronic age, you shouldn't plan to dispense with paper entirely. You'll invariably collect articles your sister-in-law tore from the newspaper, Post-it notes written at breakfast, scribblings on business cards received at meetings, flyers that come with junk mail, quotes found in fortune cookies. Drop these in the chapter folders. Don't let gems of serendipity slip away.

Think of your work as cobbling together something like the professor's taped-together remarks. Your content may still flutter loosely around the skeleton of your concept. But all the flapping shows you're getting enough material to keep your audience convinced you have what the professor stressed: evidence.

Rest assured you will build on these basic electronic and paper files later. In the meantime, you'll enjoy a big benefit: Collecting the information, especially by chapter, clarifies your thinking in yet new ways. Your grasp of message, argument, and logical flow become even stronger. You're now ready to take the fifth step on the Stairway to Earth, Right Organization.

YOUR PAPER TRAIL

STEP 4

✓ DIGITAL RESEARCH FILES

✓ PAPER RESEARCH FOLDERS

CHAPTER 5

RIGHT ORGANIZATION

See if this doesn't sound familiar: You have a week for a much-needed vacation. You rough out a plan to cover a half dozen must-see and must-do items. So enthused are you that you talk up the plan to your loved ones, gushing about the monuments, tours, shows, and the water washing over your toes at the beach.

Then you start piecing the parts together—but the pieces don't fit! The morning coastal tour leaves before your shuttle arrives. The dinner cabaret starts before the crocodile float returns. The ferry from the islands lands after the last bus leaves to connect to your flight home.

Ugh. The organization that looked so uplifting in outline now gives you a sinking feeling.

The same thing happens all the time with books. After you rough out a grand plan in your table of contents, you get excited about your argument. You're walking on air. But as you look at all the transitions, you can't quite smooth out the flow of your messages. You hit disconnects everywhere.

As with so much of life, only when you start to get into the details do you learn about the flaws in your grand plan. Such is the nature of a creative project. Fact is, you can't avoid it. But you can set aside time to regain control as you fashion the right connections.

In the last chapters, you've tested, at the highest level, the sequence of messages for your book's chapter-by-chapter argument. You've also taken time to assure that at the chapter level you have the content you need. In this step on the Stairway to

Earth, you make your argument in more detail by doing the following:

EXPLODE THE BOOK-LEVEL ARGUMENT

SECURE THE THREADS

DOCUMENT THE OUTLINE

One caution: At this stage, continue to resist the temptation to start writing. If you let yourself get pulled into composing sentences and paragraphs, you risk sidetracking yourself. By all means, if an irresistible passage jumps to mind, write it down. But to remain efficient—and preserve a fresh writing mind—stay focused on the prewriting process.

Explode the book-level argument

Imagine for a moment a parts diagram. You've seen them, those black-and-white schematics that come with everything from RadioShack gadgets to playground sets. They show how everything goes together. And if they're wrong, you think seriously about how to strangle the author.

Well, you need the same kind of parts diagram for your book. If the argument (table of contents) shows the major movement of your proposed manuscript, an exploded version shows all the pieces that go into it.

Without an outline, devilish flaws will remain hidden one or two tiers below the top-level chapter message. Not just a few nuts and bolts will be missing, but critical support pieces. Find the missing parts and flaws now and your structure won't fall down later. And you won't feel like strangling the person who did the parts diagram.

The parts diagram for a book is, of course, an outline. You need to prepare one first at the book level. Do this by breaking out three to five sub-messages for each chapter. If these messages don't clarify to your satisfaction your chapter-level argument, flesh them out further, itemizing sub-sub-messages.

Don't settle for outline entries phrased as topics instead of messages. A topic is like the name of a department in a college—biology, English, religion, engineering. It tells visitors what's studied there; it does not tell you what people there have to say. Be sure your messages show what you have to say.

Other aids for outlining:

— Answer questions: All writing answers questions. If you're having trouble with the progression of sub-messages in your outline, list questions each chapter will answer.

— Favor one-liners: The leaner the expression, the more obvious the flaws in your reasoning. In how-to books, three – to five-word imperative sentences work well. In any book, keep your messages to one line, maximum.

— Be word choosy: Seek precision in your language. Leave out adjectives and impart meaning with nouns and verbs. Wording that is "almost right" often glosses over flaws. Fuss over nuances and distinctions.

— Ignore content: Set aside your content inventory for the moment. Especially when you have juicy material, you may tend to fit your messages to content and not the other way around.

— Banish hangers on: All the material you lovingly collected will vie for your attention. Don't accommodate juicy material unless it advances your argument.

— Delay and defer: The art of argument often depends on what you say first, what you leave to later. Unbundle complex concepts to cover their component parts in the most effective order.

— Mind the close: Strong chapters, like strong movies, have a distinct start and finish. Some authors think of their start and finish as bookends. Although your bookends may not be mirror images, they can play off each other in some way—for example, the end returning to an anecdote introduced at the beginning.

If a chapter strikes you as boring, stop and try to figure out why. A sense of boredom often suggests you need to bring more insight to the material. Have you phrased the messages so you're saying something new? Boredom doesn't last long if you're confident you're engaged in a creative process.

If you get it right, expect to feel a small thrill. As you march forward with your messages, you should feel like the procession draws a few oohs and ahs from your objective self. If your inner spectator starts to fall asleep, look out. You'll never be able to drink enough coffee later to get the chapters written.

At this stage, you can't help but start thinking about what you will compose for the text. How will the first few lines in each chapter go? The opening anecdote? The summary of persuasive facts? Note thoughts that arise so you can't lose them. But avoid getting waylaid by starting to draft. For now, stay focused on perfecting your parts diagram.

Secure the threads

Now that you've gotten all your chapter messages and sub-messages down, budget time to check that they all tie together. Straighten, splice, uncoil, and re-configure as needed. If you're analytic by nature, you may do a lot of this automatically. But don't assume you do it without thinking. Set aside time to test, debug, and improve each message and transition.

As French author Gustave Flaubert said, "You speak of pearls, but pearls don't make the necklace. It's the string...Everything depends on the plan, the outline."

You can improve your outline by using all the tools you used in chapter 2. This time you use them both for individual chapters and transitions between chapters. Is your expanding argument MECE? Does it ascend a ladder of insight? Do you address two thematic levels? Did you create something elegant?

Here are other aids I find useful:

— Mind your plan: When you're working at the detail level, you can easily let one message you're chasing take you down a side path. Keep an eye on the horizon so you stay on the main trail.

— Strengthen premises: Each sub-message is a premise in your expanded argument. As you read each one, ask, Is this insightful? Can I do better? Does it drive the progression of the book forward?

— Beware fallacies (again): Don't let the strength of your passion allow you to accept weak logic. Fix misleading analogies, straw-man arguments, suppressed evidence, rationalization—anything you would roll your eyes at if you heard it from someone else.

— Favor parallelism: If you can, reuse patterns from chapter to chapter (as this book does). More often than not, this speeds the reader's comprehension. If you're writing a how-to book, favor imperatives: "Eat more bran," "Get more exercise," "Socialize more often."

— Think in threes: Minds work in threes—three acts in a play, three movements in a symphony, three bumps on a log. Limit each chapter to three messages unless you have a good reason to do otherwise. Another advantage to threes: The simpler you make your argument, the sooner you'll see the flaws and fix them.

— Jettison bad fruit: As elements of your argument mature, some notions ripen like peaches in Georgia. Others age into mush. Pay attention to the maturing process. When you realize a good idea has gone bad, set it aside.

After vetting and editing the diagrammatic view of your book, you may conclude your chapters don't flow as you would like. The chapter sequence may be wrong. Take heart, drastic change is all part of the engineering process. Dropping chapters, adding chapters, reordering them—any action is fair game to get things right before you start writing.

When I helped Bill Marquard write *Wal-Smart,* we took drastic action. The book's focus in the first half was on what Wal-Mart did to compete. The second half was on what competitors (other retailers) could do. We initially planned to write a first chapter on the demographics and characteristics of Wal-Mart shoppers. But we realized that this kickoff chapter didn't contribute to the main argument. We dropped it and integrated the material elsewhere.

Doing an overhaul at this stage of the game can be discouraging. But it's common. You can minimize the upheaval and pain, however, if you budget time for reworking your plan. Just be glad you haven't wasted any time yet on writing the manuscript.

By the way, if you're doing a narrative book—a nonfiction "novel,"—the conceptual outline I suggest here won't work. For a book like *A Civil Action,* the story about a crusading lawyer fighting toxic polluters, you need a dramatic outline. One master of this craft is Pulitzer Prize winner Jon Franklin. I recommend his *Writing for Story.*

Document the outline

To finish this step on the Stairway to Earth, create either one or two documents, depending on your book:

ELECTRONIC OUTLINE

ELECTRONIC TIMELINE

All nonfiction books demand an outline. You can start with a pencil. But as soon as you're serious, document your work electronically. As with a pencil approach, save all old documents. You never know what rubbish you squirrel away today will look to your eyes like treasure later.

I advise outlining with the outlining function in a word processor program. One of the hardest mental juggling acts in book writing is moving from the exploded view to an assembled view—or between a view of the trees and one of the forest. With an electronic outline, you can toggle instantly between the two. (Or put both side by side on a large screen.) Your mind can't do it better.

If your book has a narrative element—even if it is not a nonfiction story—another document you will probably want to create is a timeline. If you expect to relate someone's story or reconstruct an historical event, a visual chronology reveals more than you ever expect about cause and effect, and about motive and result.

The key is to use computing power to facilitate organization. The electronic outline will expand/collapse to show/hide levels of logic so you can easily keep your message top of mind even as you accumulate a vast rubble of detail. Books are gigantic projects built of endless content. You can get lost, turn in circles even, if you don't have a way to keep the lay of the land clear.

Outlining can actually be one of the more enjoyable parts of a book project. (Really!) Approached in the right way, you will see how it helps bring deeper and deeper clarification to your direction. And with every point you clarify, you take greater control of your book. You also discover new insights about your subject—and even about yourself.

You can easily make outlining frustrating if you expect handling gaps and glitches to be an easy task. But if you go into it remaining open and flexible, your acts of creativity and resourcefulness can bring out your best. You're mastering a great mental puzzle. You're also preparing yourself for your first important writing task, the book-proposal introduction. You get to that in the next, the sixth, step on the Stairway to Earth, Right Craft.

YOUR PAPER TRAIL

STEP 5

✓ELECTRONIC OUTLINE

✓ELECTRONIC TIMELINE

CHAPTER 6

RIGHT CRAFT

In museums, you often see painters copying the works of the masters. They set up their easels and mimic each of the masters' strokes. In writing, you should do something similar. Read the masters—or at least the masters of the kind of book you want to write—and study their craft.

Here's how the first chapter in a nonfiction book that has sold more than fifteen million copies opens:

> On May 7, 1931, the most sensational manhunt New York City had ever known had come to its climax. After weeks of search, "Two Gun" Crowley—the killer, the gunman who didn't smoke or drink—was at bay, trapped in his sweetheart's apartment on West End Avenue.

If one of your main jobs as a writer is to engage and hold the reader's attention, this author certainly showed how. Maybe you guessed: The author's name is Dale Carnegie. And the book is *How to Win Friends and Influence People*. First published in 1936, it still outsells most books ever published.

Every book that sells well has something to teach you. Carnegie, for example, was not successful just because he wrote better than many others of his time—although he was an excellent writer. He succeeded because he knew how to convey compelling ideas. And his mastery deserves study.

Another kind of writing to study includes nonfiction from literary masters. E. B. White, a revered essayist of the twentieth century, stood out because he could engage and hold readers' attention with insights on even trivial matters— without the help of sensational manhunts to grab readers' attention.

White wrote about things as pedestrian as receiving junk mail. From his book *One Man's Meat:*

> I got a letter from a lightening rod company this morning trying to put the fear of God in me, but with small success. Lightning seems to have lost its menace. Compared to what is going on on earth today, heaven's firebrands are penny fireworks with wet fuses.

White endeared readers for sixty years with the meaning he squeezed from slivers of ordinary living. A study of White's work (including children's books like *Charlotte's Web)* can help anyone's craft. White's work reminds us that we can always dig deeper for insights into even small experiences.

Speaking of insights, by now in the Stairway to Earth process, you have dug deeply for all the key insights you will reveal in your book. That's largely been the point of all the thinking and prewriting steps up to now. In this chapter, you take the next step in the process: Articulating those insights in the best way possible.

This chapter covers three tasks in the sixth step on the Stairway to Earth:

STUDY THE HIT PARADE

USE A VENERABLE FORM

CRAFT THE BEGINNING

Study the hit parade

If you're a professional writer, you've probably studied a lot of good writing. If not, just before you compose your next words, run your eyes over the clarity, color, contours, and textures of some fine writing. There's nothing like reading your favorites to prime yourself to write a passage that tempts, seduces, and sustains the interest of readers.

In both your competing-books research and in reading for pleasure, you will come across books you admire. Make a habit of examining key passages. What content do the authors put in the initial paragraphs? How do they arouse emotion? How do they organize paragraphs so you get the message easily? How do they keep you on track as the writing progresses?

Read books not just in your subject area. Read those using forms and language you like—the approach, structure, metaphor, and so on. A diverse reading list has a way of pulling you out of your rote phraseology and putting you in a more creative frame of mind.

In her *Pilgrim at Tinker Creek,* Annie Dillard begins:

> I used to have a cat, an old fighting tom, who would jump through the open window by my bed in the middle of the night and land on my chest...Some nights he kneaded my bare chest with his front paws, powerfully, arching his back, as if sharpening his claws, or pummeling a mother for milk. And some mornings I'd wake in the daylight to find my body covered with paw prints in blood; I looked as though I'd been painted with roses.

Arresting image. Imaginative similes. Dillard's personal narrative beckons readers to produce some extraordinary images and metaphors of their own. Writing like this can light your expository flame.

When you're reading, look especially at the following:

- Openings
- Message paragraphs
- Perspective paragraphs
- Transitions
- Closings

OPENINGS: Note how often authors use a variety of devices in the first few sentences to entice readers. Many times they tell a story—like "Two Gun" Crowley—to draw you into what happens. Or they state an insight—about junk mail—that wakes you to new meaning. Or they cite a statistic that spurs you to exclaim, "Wow!" Or they invent a figure of speech— "painted with roses"—to flash an image. Or they use questions, examples, quotes, or other means to pique your intellect or emotion. All of these are good ways to start a chapter.

MESSAGE PARAGRAPHS: Usually several lines or paragraphs into the writing, authors of serious nonfiction reveal their message. They do so in several ways: They state it explicitly, or put a quote outlining it in someone else's mouth, or explain it through example. In any case, they consciously orient you as the reader, showing the direction you are about to travel.

In her bestseller *Longitude*, Dava Sobel, opens chapter two with a story of tragedy. Rather than stating the point of her chapter in a straightforward way, she uses the story to lead readers to the message:

> ...The consensus opinion placed the English fleet [of Admiral Sir Clowdisley Shovell] safely west of Île d'Ouessant, an island outpost of the Brittany peninsula. But as the sailors continued north, they discovered to their horror that they had misgauged their longitude near the Scilly Isles...And on that foggy night of October 22, 1707, the Scillies became unmarked tombstones for two thousand of Sir Clowdisley's troops...In all, four of the five warships were lost...

> The demise of Sir Clowdisley's fleet capped a long saga of seafaring in the days before sailors could find their longitude. Page after page from this miserable history relates quintessential horror stories of death by scurvy and thirst, of ghosts in the rigging, and of landfalls in the form of shipwrecks, with hulls dashed on rocks and heaps of drowned corpses fouling the beaches. In literally hundreds of instances, a vessel's ignorance of her longitude led swiftly to her destruction.

Readers now understand why Sobel's book subtitle declares the conundrum of calculating longitude "the greatest scientific problem" of the era.

PERSPECTIVE PARAGRAPHS: Readers can misunderstand why an event or idea matters. The author has to clue them in. For example, if an individual gives an opinion, why should we give him or her credence? Is he or she famous? Was his or her outspokenness unusual in the era covered? Would the speech cause ripple effects beyond its venue? Did conditions of the era influence his or her mindset? If such questions are likely to come up in a reader's mind, good authors inject context.

In his biography of Abraham Lincoln, Henry Ketcham recognized that readers wouldn't be able to understand Lincoln if they tried to comprehend his actions without an understanding of his times. So at the beginning of *The Life of Abraham Lincoln*, he offers perspective:

"Consider now the sparseness of the population. Kentucky has an area of 40,000 square miles. One year after Lincoln's birth, the total population...was 406,511, or an average of ten persons—say less than two families—to the square mile...Illinois, with its more than 56,000 square miles of territory, harbored in 1810 only 12,282 people; in 1820, only 55,211, or less than one to the square mile..."

With the help of good saddle horses and oxen, Ketcham adds, carts could carry whiskey and other goods along roads too rough or muddy for carriages. But even by cart, little from the outside reached the people in the woods. To explain what the Lincoln family's cupboard would have looked like, Ketcham goes on:

"As to food, wild game was abundant, but the kitchen garden was not developed and there were no...oranges, lemons, bananas. No canned goods. Crusts of rye bread were browned, ground, and boiled; this was coffee. Herbs of the woods were dried and steeped; this was tea... Slippery elm bark soaked in cold water sufficed for lemonade. The milk-house, when there was one, was built over a spring when that was possible, and the milk vessels were kept carefully covered to keep out snakes and other creatures that like milk."

Paragraphs like this are often easy to create—but easy to forget to add. Do your homework and include them in your chapter early on.

TRANSITIONS: Words, sentences, paragraphs, line breaks, headings—watch how authors use them to orient and reorient the reader. The authors know that if readers can't get a fix on time, place, or the position of an argument, they will feel disoriented, and they will put a book down.

In the best cases, no overt transition is needed. One concept flows logically to the next. No extra words intercede. Other times, a single word like "meanwhile" suffices. If not, a short question may do: "But how did reporters capture Lincoln's every word?" In any case, note how authors use signposts to keep readers on the right trail.

CLOSING: Note when you run across a satisfying ending. Does it sum up the message? Hook back to the start? Offer an epilogue to a thought or event? Create a cliffhanger for the next chapter? Employ a zinger of a quote, anecdote, insight, or example to spark mental fireworks?

Consider how Dale Carnegie ended his first chapter. After profiling several desperadoes like "Two Gun" Crowley, he argued that even bad people don't think poorly of themselves. They rationalize their behavior as appropriate—rationalizing just like the rest of us do. So he closes:

> Instead of condemning people, let's try to understand them. Let's try to figure out why they do what they do. That's a lot more profitable and intriguing than criticism; and it breeds sympathy, tolerance, and kindness. "To know all is to forgive all."
>
> As Dr. Johnson said: "God himself, sir, does not propose to judge man until the end of his days."
>
> Why should you and I?

A finale like that gives readers something to reflect on and savor. See if you can learn to do the same. Watch how other authors wrap up chapters in similarly satisfying ways—and make readers desire more. The authors might cap a good argument, echo universal themes, knock on our conscience, bait us with things to come. Readers hope for, yearn for, a good close.

Use a venerable form

As you study other writing, you may continue to believe that the differences you see exceed the similarities. Authors may appear to handle concept and content opportunistically, as if one thought plays off another with no grand plan. The openings, the message statements, the perspective paragraphs—they seem to follow in unpredictable order. The author was simply being "creative."

This is ordinarily not so. Authors rarely approach their craft with a clean slate. Their writing may appear to follow a "free form," but it often reaches the page in no such structure-free way. Authors instead usually employ a repeatable form, and you would do well to do the same. The risk of writing "free form" is that you go into free fall.

So what is the repeatable form you can rely on to convey your argument? Most writers are well served by what journalists call the "feature" form. On the front page of newspapers, "news" stories generally appear. Inside and in weekend sections, you usually find "features," normally the longer and more story-like articles. In magazines, features appear in the center, news at the front. Unlike news stories, features rarely start with the "who-what-when-where-why-how" facts of a news item.

Other forms will also work for book writing, but none offers the track record of the feature form. When you have an eighty-thousand-word book to write, this time-tested way to structure writing is a useful crutch. Here are its elements:

- Lead
- Billboard or nut paragraph
- Body
- Ending

What is the lead? It is nothing more than the opening described above. The billboard or nut paragraph is nothing more than the message paragraph that states the point of the chapter. Along with the billboard comes some background to provide perspective—like Goodwin's background on Lincoln-era media.

The body is the organized presentation of the main argument of the chapter. And the ending is just that, in which you summarize your arguments, perhaps, or provide an incentive to move to the next chapter. If each chapter has these parts, each will be complete.

You may object that a reusable form will lead to too much predictability. But I advise thinking about it this way: When breaking into the ranks of authors for the first time, learn to use tools that have been proven to work reliably. You have little to risk. Once you put flesh on the bones of a repeatable writing form, most readers don't notice the form itself anyway. They just see the wonders of the clothing you hang on it.

What you put in the feature form is up to you. That's where creativity comes in. Remember that symphonies also follow a fixed form. So do short stories. You still have plenty of room for performing magic.

Your audience actually expects some form. Writers before you have conditioned them to look for it—whether your readers know it or not. Your readers, just like viewers of a movie, are watching for "plot points"—or structural fixtures they have learned to look for. Even in the simplest books, we are primed to expect the equivalent of the setup and the chase scene. If we don't get it, we may even feel cheated.

Craft the beginning

All of your study in this chapter prepares you for the next task, the first passage of writing that will, after an initial appearance in your proposal, go into your book. It may be the most important writing of all—and so justifies all you've gone through so far. I'm speaking about the introduction to your book proposal.

The introduction should contain a lead, billboard, and a transition to the body of the proposal introduction. It should begin, as in a feature article, with material as good as "Two Gun Crowley." Sometimes this material is an anecdote, sometimes an image, sometimes a naked fact, and sometimes just a plain declarative sentence or two, using vibrant words to introduce a strong concept.

If your lead hasn't done so, you next clarify your message in a billboard or "nut" paragraph. All of your thinking up to now pays off big here. Simply state what your book will say. You've already iterated this over and over. Your entire book hinges on your wording, however, so spend additional time sharpening it to a razor edge.

Try to keep your introduction under two double-spaced pages. Length does depend on what you have to say, but shoot for five hundred words or less. Remember that brevity often augments power.

Think of your proposal's introduction as the marquee on your theatre. It should draw attention like a Broadway edifice draws crowds. If you can't make your editor believe he or she absolutely *must* look inside, you have more thinking to do.

Don't write the body of the introduction. That will come later. Just focus on the beginning. The beginning is everything. End with a transition sentence to what will come next—a description of your book's approach. Here are excerpts from the beginning of the introduction to the proposal written for *The One-Minute Meditator* by David Nichol and me.

> When Paul Neary turned 66 last year, he began coming to the office a bit later every day. Problem is, he no longer got a parking space a few steps from the door. He had to park in the boonies. "It used to make me angry," he says. No matter that his walk took him across the grounds of a serene, hilltop campus carpeted with lush grass and graced with stately shade trees.
>
> Neary, a psychoanalyst and psychotherapist at the renowned Menninger Clinic in Topeka, Kansas, remained angry until he realized all at once that he had a choice—"a good surprise" he calls it. The minute or so walk from his car to the door could remain an irritant, bringing to a boil every morning his sense of indignation. Or he could view the walk as an opportunity to relieve stress through the practice of meditation...

Like Neary, many of us find that small irritants in life—let alone the bigger demands of work, family, and community—can ripple the calm of our day. We hunger to inch our way into a sort of quiet room of mental ease and stress-free living. But the moment we cross even an innocuous parking lot, all manner of perceptions, memories, feelings, and desires crash in...Our minds hang us on the rasping edge of unsatisfactoriness.

The *One-Minute Meditator* offers an antidote to this pervasive, lingering dis-ease. It administers its powerful medicine by first sketching a street map of our demanding mind. It shows the traffic of thought flowing heavily through our heads, the congestion, conflict, and gridlock provoking stress and stress-related illnesses like hypertension, headaches, and heart disease. It shows how we try to control our minds to reduce stress with half measures that don't quite work. It then offers a simple means for better mental navigating, and building an enduring sense of contentedness...

Our book focuses the reader's attention on the time span of one minute. The reason is simple. For one thing, a minute's worth of time is easy to grasp. For another, the activity of the mind is remarkably repetitive—one minute of mental activity is pretty much the same as the next...

Notice that this excerpt includes a lead, about Paul Neary. It is an anecdotal lead, aimed at stating the problem to which the book offers a solution. The lead includes a billboard, about meditation as an antidote to the kind of problem experienced by Neary. And it contains a transition to detailing the book's approach and contents.

A caution: You will feel at a disadvantage in a proposal. You haven't written the book yet, so frankly you don't have everything figured out. You are challenged to get everything just the way you want it. You may even feel uncomfortable because you're not sure you can deliver on everything. Not to worry. You can write a first draft now and iterate your way to your goals in future drafts.

In the next chapter—Stairway to Earth, Step 7: Right Game Plan—you finish the proposal. To conserve freshness, don't move to that step too quickly. Let the proposal's introduction sit for a few days. Put it away *where you can't see it.* When you've gained enough distance to be an effective self-editor, pull it out and rework it. If the masters have anything to teach, it's that the fine strokes at the end can make all the difference.

YOUR PAPER TRAIL

STEP 6

✓ PROPOSAL INTRODUCTION

CHAPTER 7

Right Game Plan

How important is the book proposal? One editor from a top New York publisher put it this way: "The book is never better than the proposal," so if the proposal is faltering, "alarm bells go off in my head." Alarm bells, that is, which tell the editor to move on to the next author's work.

If you don't want publishers to hear alarm bells, your objective should be to produce a proposal that represents your best possible work. Solve the problems in your book before you share the book idea with publishers. Use all the thinking you've done so far and then go one better. Plan to delight your prospective editor.

A proposal can falter in many ways—even more than a book—because, unlike the book, it covers more than concept and content. It is a business plan. And the publisher is a prospective investor in your work. Like any investor, the publisher wants to know you have invented something cool or useful. And he or she wants to see that it's stylish or elegant.

But that's only the beginning. The publisher wants to know it will sell.

In other words, if you are to place your book with a publishing house, you have to think of yourself as an entrepreneur. Don't make the mistake of assuming acquisition editors—the people who read proposals and make book offers—buy books just because they love them. This is rarely so. They look for gaps in marketing, distribution, publicity, and other business elements. They get so many proposals they gladly reject those with identifiable weaknesses.

So your job is simple (sort of): Don't give editors even one reason to reject your book.

You've already created all the necessary material to write your proposal. That has been the point of the last six chapters. You have even drafted an introduction. So how do you finish? How do you prepare to sell a serious nonfiction book to a publisher? I recommend the following tasks:

CHOOSE YOUR GAME

ASSEMBLE THE PIECES

DRAFT SALES DOCUMENTS

How long should a proposal be? Something upward of six thousand words, usually quite a bit more. Some authors, even veterans, write proposals of twenty-five thousand words (a third of the book!). Proposals of eight to twelve thousand words, however, generally work fine. Of this, the introduction should run no more than one thousand words.

One clarification at this point. You have probably heard of people who have written their entire book before writing a proposal. This is not a good idea. (If you are writing fiction, this is an entirely different matter.) You don't want to go to the effort of creating a product without a business plan.

The main factor in selling a book is a compelling story—a story with two parts. The first part details the "plot" of your book, that is, its conceptual argument. The second details an argument for the book's commercial success. The proposal is the masterwork that does both. You can't sell investors on a business without a master plan, and you can't sell publishers on a book without one, either.

I once advised a community dissident who had been elected on a pro-change platform to a school board and now wanted to write a book about the school system. He knew from the inside the machinations of parents' groups, PTAs, school boards, and teachers' unions. He wrote a fascinating book pinpointing ways to make schools better. He then sent query letters to editors offering it for sale. He got no response. None whatever. This is typical, and you don't want it to happen to you.

Choose your game

To write a good plan, that is, a proposal, you actually have to start thinking about the business end well before you do much writing. One decision you should weigh early on is *how* to publish. The traditional game plan is to partner with an agent who sells your proposal to a publishing house. Another is to research publishers yourself and approach them directly, as the education reformer did. A third is to self-publish, either in paper or digitally (or both).

If you take the direct route, you write publishers a one-page query letter to pitch your book. If they answer, and ask for your proposal, you're off and running. No agent required. If they buy your book, you've broken into the publishing race without an agent's 15-percent commission. This certainly can work with smaller publishers, and you may want to give it a try even for larger ones, especially if you're well connected.

Problem is, big publishers often don't respond to unsolicited queries. Most of the houses don't even accept them. If you can get the ear of an editor personally, do so. But prepare to be shut out, unless you're targeting a small publisher, in which case you should investigate approaches on a case-by-case basis.

If you want to self-publish, you have plenty of company. Authors have done so for years. *What Color is Your Parachute?* and *The One Minute Manager* were originally self-published. So were *In Search of Excellence* and many self-help and how-to books. In the Internet age, you have more options than ever to self-publish, and many are cheap. You can even dispense with paper altogether and publish an e-book. Check out the possibilities with Amazon and Smashwords.

Some self-published books sell in huge quantities. That's often because the authors not only have a good idea but they know how to market and sell. If a self-published book is successful, mainstream publishers may even buy publishing rights, which means they then use their distribution power to get it in bookstores everywhere. But do-it-yourself success comes to few authors. If you do decide to take this approach, check out the many books and websites that will advise you on the specifics.

In this book, I advocate finding an agent. To my mind, an agent is the best way to reach a mainstream publisher. Agents know the market. They know the editors. They know how to negotiate. The know how to advise you on how to win.

As with a publisher, unfortunately, you may have trouble getting one.

I suggest going with a publisher as opposed to self-publishing. Most serious authors desire the vetting, editorial expertise, distribution power, and imprimatur of a publisher. Going it alone as you write a book is hard enough. Going it alone with editing, publishing, marketing, and distribution is doubly so. If you choose that route, be sure you're up to the do-it-yourself regimen.

In any case, weigh your options before you write your proposal. If you're self-publishing, you can of course skip the formal document. But I suggest you go through the motions. Address all the elements so you have done all the thinking, all the prewriting, and produce a complete plan. Executing the plan will fall entirely on your shoulders.

A confession. Having published all my previous books with mainstream publishers, I decided to publish this one myself. At first I tried to sell it to a publishing house directly, but when I got no response on the first round of queries, I decided to experiment with self-publishing. So you hold in your hands an experiment—an experiment in writing and business—and I will report on my Stairway to Earth blog what I learn from it.

Assemble the pieces

Most of the content you need for a proposal, and the basis for its business sections, sits in your inventory of electronic documents. This should come as a relief. Just as the pressure ramps up for you to produce smart sound bites to impress investors, you can pull material off the shelf. Your cupboard is jammed.

Like a book, a proposal can be written in any format or order you please. But editors, like venture capitalists, are used to getting plans in a familiar form. Inventing a new mousetrap may not improve your odds of success. It may force the editor to fumble with a new contraption.

Here are the standard proposal sections (the order varies):

- Introduction
- Market for the book

- Competing books
- Book positioning
- Marketing plan
- Author platform
- About the author
- Work plan
- Table of contents
- Chapter summaries
- Sample chapter

Some editors like to see a list of sales points, too. The sales points answer the question all publishers' sales people will ask: If I'm going to pitch the book to buyers—that is, to the purchasing people who buy inventory for stores—what should I say to sell the book?

A publisher's salesperson might have thirty seconds to pitch a book. Your sales points arm him or her with talking points. These points should be in your proposal's marketing and positioning sections. But if you feel you need to highlight the sales argument in your business plan, break them out into a separate list.

Here are more tips for preparing the material for each section of a proposal:

INTRODUCTION: Relook at the lead and billboard in your introduction. Are they just right? Do they say the right thing and say it in the right way? Next, have you amply clarified in your mind a summary of the book's contents, its differentiating features, your unique qualities as the author, your marketing and sales plans?

In general, ask yourself: How can I highlight the book's premier selling points? Prepare to put a brief answer in the section following your lead.

MARKET FOR BOOK: For the section devoted just to the book's market, your foremost task is to quantify the size of your core audience. An example: Say your book is about dog psychiatry. Ask: How many dog owners have dogs that need mental health services? How many books (of related kinds) have sold to them? Compile Nielsen BookScan figures, book-ranking numbers from online booksellers, and relevant sales figures from titlez.com.

Be creative in finding ways to quantify the audience, but if you don't have solid numbers, look for ways to describe qualitatively your audience's character, scale, and scope. Even if you believe it, don't say your market is "huge." Nobody will believe you. You have to honestly and soberly profile your core readership. Only in brief should you investigate and plan to characterize other audiences that may cross over to buy your work.

The proposal has to answer the twenty-thousand-copies question: Where are twenty thousand book buyers who will pay $25 for my book (or $14.99 or $19.99 or whatever)? Books don't make a handsome profit for publishers until sales hit twenty thousand copies. Truth be known, many books don't sell more than five thousand copies, and big publishers won't buy books that promise a paltry market.

COMPETING BOOKS: Identify at least a half dozen of the books most likely to compete with yours. Prepare a list of titles with author, publisher, date, and sales data. Do not overlook any titles that would compete with you head to head. Be thorough. Remember, too, that competition is not all bad: It shows you have a market.

BOOK POSITIONING: Review and highlight notes in your positioning journal (from chapter 3). Which passages best explain how your book differs from others? Which ones say why it is better? Choose the strongest language and go one better to make your case persuasively.

Remember to look for books to compare with yours in catchy ways. Comparisons can give you an all-important handle. If you say your book is the *Men Are from Mars, Women Are from Venus* of dog psychology, you have something to hook an editor's attention in a snap. They can grasp without a lot of added description the world the book opens up for readers.

MARKETING PLAN: Business people often use the terms "marketing channels" and "sales channels" to denote the avenues through which you publicize, promote, create buzz, and sell. Your "channels" may include control of a website, seminar circuit, or appearances on talk shows. Or they may include access to an e-mail list, an inside track with a retail chain, or just a list of personal contacts. For your proposal, itemize channels you already control. If they are weak, note those you can develop.

Contrary to popular belief, although publishers help with book-launch publicity, they often don't do much more. And if point-of-sale data show your book isn't taking off, they may quickly pull all the marketing chips off your table, shifting them to proven winners. So take time to think through an independent marketing program.

As for marketing channels, will you advertise in your online newsletter? Do a direct (junk) mailing? Speak from a soapbox on street corners in New York? As for sales channels, will you run an online bookstore? Will you distribute through retail pet shops? Will you sell books from a display table at dog shows?

Truth be known, publishers tend to take a winners-take-all approach. They give big sellers all the marketing money. If you're not a star baseball player, rock star, or famous (or infamous) politician, you get the leftovers. Be prepared to run your own show.

AUTHOR PLATFORM: What is a "platform"? It is the sum total of the marketing and sales channels you control. I break out platform as a separate heading because it alone can make or break your proposal.

Do you give keynote speeches? Run seminars and workshops? Host a radio show? Run a Fortune 500 company? Write your core audience's most popular blog? Buy hundreds of books in bulk for your company?

Can you sell books at conferences? If you're a professor, can you get colleges to "adopt" your book? Does your sister run a retail empire that will put your book at a thousand checkout counters?

The bigger your platform, the better your chances of success with a publisher. Spend plenty of time thinking this through.

ABOUT THE AUTHOR: Along with "platform," a crucial question for publishers is your "authority." Your authority comes from credentials, reputation, capabilities, and accomplishments. Why are you qualified and respected? Why are you the go-to person on this subject?

Publishers don't just buy books; they buy authors. So why are you fit to become the publisher's next partner? What leads the publisher to believe you can write your book, deliver it on time, and promote the heck out of it? Do you have stage and screen presence? Can you make videos to post on the web to spur sales?

WORK PLAN: How much work have you done? What's left to do? How long will it take? Prepare an estimate. You will be able to negotiate later.

TABLE OF CONTENTS: Relook at your chapter titles and subtitles. Will they grab a reader?

CHAPTER SUMMARIES: Prepare material to summarize the contents of each chapter. One good format is to start each summary with a chapter lead and billboard. You can then transition to a conventional summary of chapter contents.

If you've been following the Stairway to Earth process up to now, you already have three to five sub-messages per chapter. Review these and prepare to list all of them and give a sampling of one or two compelling content items for each. Say you're doing that dog psychology book and including a case on a manic Shetland sheepdog named Ranger. Devise a way to give the reader a taste of Ranger's story.

SAMPLE CHAPTER: Though not all proposals require one, assume you will have to include a sample chapter. A "sample chapter" is not often a full chapter. It is a reasonable facsimile, usually on the short side. It's long enough to show you can write. Choose a chapter that, once written, will show you at your best. If you're a writer with a track record—a journalist, say—ask your agent if you need a sample chapter at all. Your proposal may be all that you need.

Draft sales documents

Now that you've marshaled all the material for a proposal, sit down and write it. If you don't have good material to lead each chapter summary, you may want to resort to pencil-and-tablet doodling. But normally the process of assembling the pieces will give you the time needed to formulate language for each proposal section.

Remember this has to be a best effort. Your target is a draft that's 70 percent right. You already have a draft of your introduction's lead, so you have a head start. Now for the rest of the sections, if you can't come up with words that take you 70 percent of the way before drafting, go back a step. Give yourself more time to ruminate. Write only when you feel words welling up from the passion you have for your message.

Remember that everything rides on your performance. If you can't sell your proposal to a publisher, you don't even get to write the book. Remember, too, that you're not just selling your book to an acquisition editor. The editor uses the proposal to sell it to an editorial board—which includes marketing, sales, and other people. They make a decision jointly. And the board won't support a book they don't totally believe in.

When I first wrote books for other people, I learned the trade from a widely admired Boston-based editorial consultant. I often wrote rough drafts of proposals, and the consultant, Donna Carpenter, used to say that our book proposals had to be so persuasive that a reader would exclaim, "I have to have this book or I will die!"

On every book since, Donna's words have echoed in my head. I ask, Does the proposal make me feel that way? Does the book sound not just provocative but positively essential? Is it a must-read? A got-to-have? Do I wish like crazy that the book was already written so I could read it *tonight*?

After you finish the proposal, you have one more item to add to your paper trail: a pitch letter. Whether you use an agent or not, draft a letter pitching your book to an editor. You are creating an elevator pitch that you will use over and over, even if you never send the letter. Draft it last because it has to reflect all the thinking you've gone through to this point.

The pitch letter is a lot like your précis. You might even want to take out your précis and consult it. Note how your thinking has advanced, however. The foundation of your pitch is your message, elaborated into the problem, solution, and benefits. Or into the subject, chronology, climax, and meaning. Add a few sentences about yourself, your market, and your platform. Keep it to one page.

Make the pitch as provocative as you can. To the extent that your publisher is your investor, highlight how your partnership will pay dividends. Don't give acquisition editors a reason to file your book in the recycling bin even before they get the proposal. If you have an agent, he or she can use your pitch to draft their own letter.

To win with the business parts of your proposal, keep in mind your role as entrepreneur. As that editor from that top New York publishing house said, "Ask not what your publisher can do for you, but what you can do for them." It's up to you to deliver the goods.

With that in mind, take a peek ahead to the next chapter. You might want to at least think about Stairway to Earth, Step 8, Right Work Program, as you write your proposal. Indeed, if you get on the phone with an editor—what you hope for after you or your agent has sent your query letter—he or she will want to start talking deadlines. Be prepared.

YOUR PAPER TRAIL

STEP 7

✓BOOK PROPOSAL

✓PITCH LETTER

CHAPTER 8

RIGHT WORK PROGRAM

Winston Churchill, who won a Nobel Prize in literature in 1953, once said, "Writing a book was an adventure. To begin with, it was a toy, an amusement, then it became a mistress, then a master, and then a tyrant."

However much fun books are to contemplate, they don't remain a toy or amusement for long. They require discipline. So the question is, How do you master the book, instead of the book mastering you?

There is no magic. Managing a book project has a lot in common with project management of any kind. You have to organize your tasks, figure out what to run in parallel and what to run in sequence, and schedule time for everything to come together by the deadline.

One of the hardest mental barriers to creating a realistic work program is simply accepting that a book takes a long time to write. It takes hundreds and hundreds of hours. And before you know it, the hundreds can become a thousand—and maybe more.

While writing my first bylined trade book, I made a big mistake. I agreed to write the book in six months because, off the cuff, that seemed like plenty of time. Only after signing the contract did I divvy up the roughly twenty-four weeks among eleven chapters, subtracting some prescheduled vacation, and allotting time for notes, acknowledgements, and fact checking.

I can still remember the shock. And the sinking feeling. I knew how long it took me to write each seven-thousand-word chapter—more like three weeks, instead of the two weeks I now had. With such a deadline, I realized that life as I knew it was ending. Indeed, I started writing before dawn and finished well after sunset for weeks.

The lesson is this: Even when you've written books before, it's hard to accept that so many months will go by before you have a publishable manuscript. Unless you set your expectations and schedule realistically, your book can become your tyrant.

I advise two simple tasks in this final step on the Stairway to Earth:

BUDGET WORK HOURS

DRAFT A SCHEDULE

Pretty simple. But these steps are so important that you should not try to do them in your head or on a napkin. Address them methodically, and commit them to printable documents, as you have the rest of your work in the book-writing process. Your reward will be greater peace of mind and more success in meeting deadlines.

Wait a minute. The last step on the Stairway to Earth? Yes, by the end of this chapter you will have done all the work to get your ideas out of the clouds., You'll have finished the prewriting and, as I like to say on my Website, be ready to "hit the ground...writing"—that is, ready to proceed with the manuscript. The second half of the book will be the Road to Publication.

Budget work hours

If your proposal works its magic, you will hook the interest of several editors. They may want to talk by phone, and they may want to present your idea to an editorial committee. If the committee buys in, you get a phone offer. If you accept, you get a long, dense contract. This is a great feeling!

But that's when reality hits: The contract includes a hard deadline. How do you get the work done?

To begin with, you should anticipate this step early on. You should probably start on it before you prepare your proposal. You'll then have a better idea of how to negotiate the deadline during your oral offer—or renegotiate it during contract talks.

Here are the hours I budget for an eight-chapter, sixty-thousand-word manuscript of serious nonfiction. I offer this budget as an example, not as a guideline for your particular book. Every book has its own requirements. Depending on your book it could take half as much time (unlikely) or twice as much (more likely).

Time budget for précis and table of contents

Reading background	1 week
Drafting précis and table of contents	1 week
Total	2 weeks, 80 hours

Time budget for proposal

Reading more background	1.5 weeks
Fresh research and interviewing	1 week
Draft initial proposal sections	1 week
Draft eight chapter summaries	2.5 weeks
Rework/edit proposal	1 week
Total	7 weeks, 280 hours

Time budget for manuscript

Refine approach (per publisher)	1 week
More research for 8 chapters	3 weeks
Final research/drafting per chapter	3 weeks (24 total)
Draft introduction/afterword	2 weeks
Rewrite eight chapters (@2+ days each)	3 weeks
Edit each chap and intro (@2 days each)	3 weeks
Edit entire book per your editor	3 weeks
Total	39 weeks, 1,560 hours
Grand total	48 weeks, 1,920 hours

You'll notice that I broke the budgeting process into three parts; précis, proposal, and manuscript. Although the process has many more steps, I find that these make useful milestones in thinking through and executing a book project. Each ends with a sense of closure, and so also makes a convenient chunk in which to budget your time.

The figures assume you're writing a book you know something about, not a book for which your have zero material. It also assumes that you still have a chunk of research to do. Note, too, that the figures are for working time, not calendar time, and are for forty-hour weeks.

To avoid the mistake I made, don't assume you have a grip on your timeline before estimating your work hours for each task individually. The tally of hours for completing a publishable manuscript will add up fast. You may even feel embarrassed to admit to others how long you think it will take (I always do). But trust your math, not your gut.

You might ask, How could it possibly take so long? I ask myself this each time. But the weeks add up. If you're writing a narrative book, you will need more time, months more, owing to more research. This budget, for example, includes only three weeks of research on the book as a whole before starting chapter-specific research. Often you will need three months.

Even if you're an authority in your field, a book may take longer than you think. One reason is that a book-length linear argument with a sustained progression of insights takes a lot of time to figure out. Another is that, like most professionals, you will probably use the book not just to document your insights but to advance them. The process of pushing your thinking to a new level is exciting but time-consuming.

Draft a schedule

The time budget can be misleading as a guide to scheduling. Taken alone, it implies that working time equals calendar time. But this is rarely the case. For one thing, you will take time off, if only to tend to the needs of family and friends. For another, you will be waiting at various junctures for your editor's comments, and he or she will need turnaround time.

So after you do a time budget, prepare a schedule. Make adjustments for holidays, vacation, and other time away. If you work hard to make up for holidays, omit them in your schedule. If you plan to "work" during holiday weeks, be wary. You should still take that time out of your schedule if you know you'll be repeatedly pulled away from work.

To see how a schedule might look, assume your New Year's resolution is to start your book. On Monday, January 2, you shake off your holiday daze and get your desk cleared. You sharpen pencils. You muse over and toy with your message. About mid-month, you finally go full time. Here's what your schedule might look like:

Milestone	Deadline
PRÉCIS/TABLE OF CONTENTS	FEBRUARY 1
PROPOSAL RESEARCH	FEBRUARY 19
PROPOSAL DRAFT	MARCH 15
PROPOSAL REVISIONS	MARCH 22
AGENT SALE/BOOK CONTRACT	MAY 17*
GENERAL RESEARCH	JUNE 14
CHAPTER 1	JULY 5
CHAPTER 2	JULY 26
CHAPTER 3	AUGUST 16
CHAPTER 4	SEPTEMBER 6
CHAPTER 5	SEPTEMBER 27
CHAPTER 6	OCTOBER 18
CHAPTER 7	NOVEMBER 8
CHAPTER 8	NOVEMBER 29
INTRODUCTION/EPILOGUE	DECEMBER 13
SECOND DRAFT	JANUARY 17 (MS TO PUBLISHER)
THIRD DRAFT	FEBRUARY 14 (MS TO PUBLISHER)
PUBLICATION	DECEMBER 14**

* = ASSUMES TWO-MONTH TURNAROUND TIME TO SELL BOOK TO PUBLISHER.

** = ASSUMES NINE-MONTH PUBLISHING TURNAROUND TIME.

The turnaround time by your editor can vary from a couple of weeks to a couple of months. He or she will probably read your manuscript twice, at two different times. You can often use this time productively for housekeeping tasks—fact checking, permissions, art or photo development. But you won't be making any progress on your manuscript.

This schedule includes only one week for your editor to turn around the first two drafts of your manuscript. If he or she takes more time, you have to extend the schedule. Included in the schedule is also a two-month turnaround to sell your proposal and a nine-month turnaround for publication. Both are typical, although they could be shorter.

Most "mid-list" books, those not by top-selling authors, enter a nine-month production schedule. The publisher, in other words, takes nine months from manuscript submittal to manufactured (or electronic) book. With today's technology, that could be (and sometimes is) radically shorter. But publishers ordinarily work on this longer schedule, owing to editorial and marketing processes unrelated to technology.

Why so long? I won't explain all the reasons. But let me give just one example of the time expended. Publishers send cheap copies of your book—called "galleys" or "proof copies"— to reviewers three months before publication. The book, though essentially done, sits around while book reviewers have the time to read the book, write a review, and enter it into their own magazine production schedules. Such steps consume weeks of lead time. Usually, you just have to accept them as part of the schedule.

You can press your publisher for faster turnaround—maybe six months. All the better, so long as you don't sacrifice quality and marketing effort. But, as the author, realize that once you submit the final manuscript, you have more work of your own to do—filling in gaps, preparing a notes section, writing the acknowledgments, mounting a marketing campaign. You may actually appreciate some of this time.

In any case, your main challenge at this point is keeping yourself on schedule. Although the publisher may cause delays, you're more likely to cause them yourself. So as you prepare your schedule, make a realistic one. Then plan to meet it. In some ways, that's all that separates a professional writer from an amateur—reliably delivering on time.

You can use your schedule to help you do this. Writers often give in to the temptation of using too much time on early chapters and then coming up short on later ones. To avoid this, think of your time budget as a bank account. When you have spent the last dime designated for one deliverable, you simply have to move onto the next. No loans!

My view is that you are better off delivering 70 percent on each deliverable than getting only 70 percent of the book done by the final deadline. I will explain later why taking this approach can also increase your overall efficiency. In the meantime, note that if you don't meet the manuscript deadline, your publisher can cancel your contract.

As a ballpark figure for a "concept" book, I assume the job will take a year. If you do it in half the time (as I did for the book you're reading), it's because you know the subject cold and you're not writing a long book. You also have an ample concept and the content. If you take twice that time, you're working on a longer or more complex book.

Many people get behind schedule, I believe, because they think of a book too much as a creative enterprise. Yes, it is very creative. Shaping concepts, fitting content to concepts, making the argument sing—these all take innovation and invention. And they take time! But the job of book writing requires putting a collar on creation and getting on with the craft.

Writing is not unlike other activities also called "arts." Tchaikovsky once said he had "a quite cold, deliberate, technical process of work." He didn't always feel creative. "An honest artist cannot sit with his hands crossed because he is not inclined to compose," he wrote. "If one waits for inclination, instead of advancing to meet it, one easily drifts into laziness and apathy."

The schedule and other devices in the Stairway to Earth process help you "advance to meet your inclination." In some ways, the schedule is your metronome. Stay on beat. You will get yourself to the bottom of the Stairway to Earth on schedule, and you will then go on to steadily advance through the six steps on the Road to Publication, the subject of the remainder of this book.

YOUR PAPER TRAIL

STEP 8

√TIME BUDGET

√BOOK SCHEDULE

PART 2

The Road to Publication

CHAPTER 9

RETOOL

People often liken writing a book to giving birth. If only it were so! After the searing pain of hours of labor, the product would normally come out perfect, beautiful, and fully formed. The package would be complete.

But producing a book isn't like that at all. Big, creative projects never come out perfect, beautiful, or complete the first time. They are imperfect, forlorn, and lame. At delivery, the product is an approximation. A prototype. A crudely carved first pass.

With a proposal in hand, you may have thought (should have thought) you had a book concept with all its essential parts. But after a few weeks, as you have time to rotate it in your mind, you see it for what it is: A work-in-process model.

Wouldn't it be nice if we could turn out masterpieces on the first pass? "Do it right the first time," would be the dictum. Book writing, however, just doesn't work that way—at least not for most of us. (A better dictum would be: "Do it right the *last* time"—because that's the only one that counts to readers.)

Note that during the book-writing process, you should *aim* to deliver everything right the first time. But you can't reasonably expect to give birth to that perfect child. Writing a book is more like producing software. The proposal is release 0.5, the first draft, release 1.0. In between you produce a number of successively better, bug-free iterations.

To get to release 1.0 of the manuscript, I suggest starting with three tasks. This is the first step on the Road to Publication, and it comes after the proposal.

ITERATE YOUR OUTLINE, ONE CHAPTER AT A TIME

VALIDATE YOUR OUTLINE, ONE CHAPTER AT A TIME

DOCUMENT YOUR WORK

This and the next three phases of book development—including those phases covered in chapters 10, 11, and 12—require shifting your work focus. Up to now, you've labored over your entire book. You've taken a macro, holistic approach. How will all the messages in the book line up to give a knockout punch? Now you switch to working on one chapter at a time, taking a micro, piecework approach.

In other words, you take all of your chapters, one at a time, through the tasks of retooling, researching, writing, and editing. After completing your final chapter, you then have your first complete, printable manuscript. In chapter 13, you return to taking a macro view, working on the flow of the whole book.

So now, turn your attention to your first chapter. Start by reviewing the thought processes in chapters 2 (argument) and 5 (organization). It's time to use these processes again to retune the argument and elaborate each chapter's organization, that is, iterate each chapter's outline. This will be part of a continuous improvement process that moves you from the proposal's facsimile to a first draft.

Iterate the chapter outline

An easy way to get started with this phase is to go to your book-length outline and cut and paste your first chapter into a new, separate document. Don't worry about all the other chapters at this point. Just take one at a time. You can't, of course, forget about the chapters you're not working on. But you can compartmentalize your work to make it manageable.

So, starting with chapter 1 (not the introduction, which comes later), rework any awkwardness that you can now see in your three to five messages. When you get the top-level messages to flow, elaborate them in greater detail—that is, explode the parts diagram down to the nuts and bolts. This may require third – or even fourth-level headings.

In the chapter outline, you are giving yourself your final marching orders for writing. Make them unmistakable! Imagine you're writing how-to directions for a friend. The clearer the orders for lead, billboard, and message points, the easier the work will go.

If you get the feeling that something isn't quite right, resist the urge to gloss over, move on, and defer. Deal with the discomfort on the spot. You don't want to discover convolutions in the driving directions after you've embarked on writing—and gone too far down the wrong road with your manuscript.

Beware of letting your argument bloat. Do flesh out its full musculature, but aim for a lean body. You may be tempted to add pet ideas that drift off message. But resist this urge. Recognize that a book, even a big one, covers a lot less than you think, and if you want to cover it well, you have to leave the pets behind.

Validate your outline

To be sure your concept holds up, perform some "tests" on it. Like a software programmer, run it through your mind and check for bugs. Where does the message flow get twisted? Where does the rigor of the reasoning fall short of your standards? Before you declare the outline of each chapter done, try the following:

ACCURACY: Ask again, Is my message "right"? That is, have you stated it correctly? Once again, don't let eloquence be the enemy of accuracy. Make sure your messages follow your book's specific thread, not a related one. If, say, you're writing about loyalty, you may talk a lot about trust. But be wary of letting your train of thought on trust derail your train of logic on loyalty. Your reader will expect you to keep the two separate.

FLOW: Ask again, Do the concepts move easily and in sequence from one to the next? Do I have a continuous river of thought, or do backwaters impede the flow? Sometimes the best way to speed the flow is simply to drop a favorite sub-message that gets in the way. If a backwater of material brings your progression of insights to a halt, call a time-out to question whether the material should even be in the book.

My recent book, *Merchants of Virtue,* chronicles the journey of one big company in its quest for sustainability (green and good). The company, furniture maker Herman Miller, grew into a premiere brand based on its high-end designs. I included a background chapter on design, which seemed to me to provide logical context. But my editor, after she saw what I wrote, told me my chapter treatment halted the narrative on sustainability. I had to rework the chapter, cutting an entire section and adding another that related better to sustainability. If you can, you want to avoid this kind of painful detour.

BALANCE: Check for balance among your sections. Do acts 1, 2, and 3 in your conceptual story get roughly the same weight? Bulk up or merge weak sections and scale down or break up overloaded ones. As in a symphony or movie or theatre play, you should provide a balanced performance, one movement or episode or act at a time.

UNITY: Does every point serve the main message? Is the chapter's flow of conceptual contents MECE (mutually exclusive and collectively exhaustive)? Does the chapter hold together while holding to the theme?

CLARITY: Does jargon camouflage vague thinking? Are the analogies and metaphors apt? Complex language, metaphor, and jargon can all too easily paper over cracks in logic.

Authors who propose to convert PhD theses or academic papers into trade books should especially take note. Though jargon from their specific fields, on the surface, seems more precise than lay language, I often find it is less. When you parse the concepts, you find the jargon often conflates vital distinctions. Using lay language can actually sharpen thinking.

After running these tests, retool your argument. If you do it now, you can possibly avoid the kind of rewrites—and anxious moments—that come with the kind of eleventh-hour reworking I did on *Merchants of Virtue*.

As part of the retooling, I recommend you improve your outline on at least three other fronts. First, improve symmetry or parallelism. Expressing thoughts in similar ways, often with similar sentence construction, makes them easier to grasp. So ask: Are like concepts expressed in like form? Or am I bringing in needless variety that hampers comprehension? If you're writing about tennis, for example, word all your message points similarly: Move to the ball, swing all the way through, take a deep breath before serving.

Why are lists of do's and don'ts so popular? Because the language is all parallel, instantly graspable.

Say you're writing a book about how to improve education, and it's for parents. You have itemized five actions that can be variously taken by parents, school boards, PTA members, teachers, or administrators. But you realize: My statements are not parallel. The actor in each action is different. Is there any way to make them all the same? (You actually have two problems: a lack of parallelism and a failure to address your targeted readers.)

You can fix this problem if you express what parents can do for each item, even if they don't hold the most authority for that particular task. For instance, you might change "School boards should require state testing" to "Parents should lobby school boards to require state testing." You cast parents as the subject of each sentence, creating a parallelism, and in turn more directly showing your targeted audience what each of them has the power to do.

Second, reduce abstraction. Even though you state chapter sub-messages as concepts, you want to express them in a down-to-earth way. I like how songwriters sometimes refer to simple but potent songs as "three chords and the truth." If you write sub-messages using complex "chords" and abstract "truths" they may have a foggy, muddled sound. When it comes time to write, you may not even remember exactly what you meant.

Say your chapter describes the role of parents in helping students handle social conflicts. You start with, "Use positive approaches to resolve problems." What does "positive" mean? What "problems" are you talking about? (The words "positive" and "problem" always raise a red flag.) A more concrete message might be, "Coach students to choose different behavior." Sub-messages might be, "Listen actively," "Ask clarifying questions," "Add facts," "Solicit alternatives," "Check on progress."

Third, express concepts in a way that matters to readers emotionally. You can hook readers emotionally faster than you can hook them intellectually. To set the emotional hook, evoke images and ideas from human experience. Work to evoke empathy.

Say you're writing a chapter on academic testing. You could write about the flaws in the tests—how they put some ethnic groups at a disadvantage, or how they undercut broad and rich school curricula. Consider instead framing your messages to express the effect on kids, even giving an account of one kid's story. Journalists do this all the time, using local stories to illustrate global ideas. Your writing then does double duty—appealing to your readers' heads and hearts.

Authors of serious nonfiction books occasionally skip the how-to approach and turn their message into novel-like parables. Dry points on management or human relations then jump to life. William Lederer and Eugene Burdick adopted this approach in the classic *The Ugly American.* Kenneth Blanchard and Spencer Johnson took it in perennial best seller *The One Minute Manager.* Both are fiction based on fact. Lederer and Burdick revealed the failings of the U.S. diplomatic corps. Blanchard and Johnson illustrated timeless principles of managing and motivating people.

While you're at it, ask yourself whether your book ties to universal themes. *The One Minute Manager,* on the surface, tells a story of management. But it became a best seller because it really tells a story of universal principles of life.

Singer Arlo Guthrie was once asked whether he wrote for the benefit of "social change." Most of his fans would say that he certainly did. That was his trademark. But Guthrie replied that he didn't think of his work that way at all. Instead, he wrote for social continuity. You will write a stronger book if whatever "new" thing you're writing about springs from all those "old" things that make up the bedrock of daily life.

Document your work

Be sure to document all your iterations. If you change your chapter outlines significantly, create new documents and save your old ones for later reconsideration. You should end up with two items for guiding the rest of your writing for each chapter.

CHAPTER OUTLINE

REFINED CHAPTER NUT OR BILLBOARD

You might wonder if these chapter-by-chapter outlining and validation tasks are necessary. Don't you already have a good outline and nut in your proposal? Don't you already know your three to five chapter points? Why not get right to writing? The answer is that experience shows few people think clearly enough to get their thinking done in the proposal. And if they have the luck to do so, they are dissatisfied with their first best effort anyway. That's because, before they begin, they want to move their game to a higher level.

In *The One-Minute Meditator*, David Nichol and I quoted Meister Eckhart, the thirteenth-century philosopher and mystic: "The soul grows by subtraction, not by addition..." Eckhart wasn't talking about writing, of course, but he could have been. When you relook at something after setting it aside for a while, a funny thing happens. You see how taking things out makes an argument stronger. You may even toss out gems you once thought essential. Only time gives you this perspective.

In the process of refining your chapter outline, take time to refine the chapter nut statement. A good proposal will state each chapter's nut absolutely clearly. But again, with time, the mind will allow you to drop unnecessary parts and identify missing nuances. When you're done refining it, embed the nut at the start of your chapter outline. It is now truly the billboard to your chapter.

If you're using a timeline to help you deal with your book's chronology, you have another task at this point. In the same way you refine your outline, refine the timeline. Add notes, amend dates, look for cause and effect you couldn't see earlier. You'll find it effective to toggle between timeline and outline, the insights from one often suggesting revisions to the other.

Now is a good time to think about word count. In your book contract, you will have agreed on a count for the entire book. Let's assume you agreed to write a ten-chapter book of sixty thousand words. That means you agreed to roughly six thousand words per chapter. Now as you refine your outline, allocate a share of the six thousand words to each chapter section.

Say your chapter has a long lead, three major sections, and a closing. One possible allocation: 1,500 words to each major section, 750 to the lead, and 750 to the close. Total: 6,000. Does this make sense given your outline? Did you expect to have more than 1,500 words for each of your messages? If so, the word count may point to further revisions. Did you expect to have less? Perhaps this points to the need for more research.

In practice, no book gets sliced up into neat six thousand-word packages. But doing a "copyfit," as journalists call it, tells you how to scale both your research and writing. Invariably, you will have imagined that one of your favorite topics will fill many pages. But when you look at your allocated word count, poof! You realize you don't really have the space. Time to abridge.

As you retool your outline, you will trigger new flashes of insight. If you want to include them, now is the time, before you've written yourself out of room. In an interview, West Virginia songwriter Kathy Mattea had some advice about creativity that applies in this phase. She said that she always starts songwriting with an intent, but when the song begins developing, she gets out of the way. She lets the song steer her.

"I think our job as creative people is to be fearless about that," she said, "and not hold onto the original thought too hard, not hold any of it too hard and [instead] to let it evolve." That's true enough of book writing. Start with an original thought. Iterate. Add research. Evolve.

And when you get to research, look ahead to the next chapter, the second step on the Road to Publication. You are now at the point where you need to match your refined messages with worthy evidence. You are well prepared: You know just what you want to say, and you know just how much space you have to express yourself. You should feel a ripple of excitement. You're closing in on the preparation of your manuscript.

YOUR PAPER TRAIL

STEP 9

✓ CHAPTER OUTLINE

✓ REFINED NUT PARAGRAPH

CHAPTER 10

RESEARCH

I once worked with a group of writers who, like so many professionals, sometimes had to kill a promising project. After so much effort, people (like me) would groan, "What a waste of work!" To which one of our senior writers would snap, "There's no such thing as wasted work."

Yuh, sure, I'd mutter. But she was onto something. As you explore new ideas, develop concepts, and invent metaphors, the creative effort of writing doesn't go to waste. Even if the project dies, the raw material lives on, compost for a new garden.

The same can't be said when it comes to book research. In a world of limited time, once you complete a conceptual outline, there *is* wasted work. The waste stems from gathering the wrong content. Or floundering over what to look for. Or getting far more than you need. Research can be fun, but it can turn into an indulgence.

One of the reasons for a refined outline is to identify research targets. What game are you hunting for? For which chapter? When you settle on your word count, you can actually calculate roughly how many sentences you have to write for each section. And when you know the sentence count, you can size your research task.

To be sure, writing is not so mechanical. Still, once you get to this stage in a book's development, your final deadline will loom on the horizon. And your desire to work efficiently will overshadow your urge to satisfy curiosity. Think of this phase as the right moment to hang up the artist's beret and roll up your sleeves: It's time to go to work on the shop floor of book writing.

The job you face now is to find just the right content, of just the right quality, and position it in just the right place to build a chapter efficiently. If you've worked on a factory floor, you might see the parallels with "just-in-time" production. People on today's shop floors don't stockpile raw materials and parts just in case they need them for a big order. They acquire the materials and parts at just the right time to fill a customer's order.

The objective, on the shop floor as well as in the writer's seat, is to reduce waste. Waste in time. Waste in unused material. Waste in rework from rehashing the wrong material. Waste in replacing what you've misplaced.

If you do an effective job of research, you don't come up with too little, and thus get stuck with weak content. And you don't come up with too much, and so misappropriate your time. Instead, you conjure up the Goldilocks effect—ample material to choose from without leaving a pile of perfectly good, unused material.

I suggest three tasks in this second step on the Road to Publication:

PREPARE A RESEARCH CHECKLIST

FINISH YOUR RESEARCH

ORGANIZE FOR JUST-IN-TIME ACCESS

Prepare a research checklist

Once you finish a chapter outline, you have a complete conceptual train of thought. With a glance, you can see where you have gaps. Your simple task now is to prepare a checklist and note what content—evidence—you have to go after.

This is an extension of chapter 4, Right Content, in which you identified and earmarked content you had on hand. Your earlier work, though, was cursory, and you focused on feasibility. Your current work is rigorous, and you focus on follow through. In chapter 4, you may have had just a foggy idea of where content fit. Now you figure out the fit exactly.

Finish your research

Look for a mix of interesting and intriguing material to finish your research. Draw it from professional journals, site visits, interviews, observation at events, studies and surveys, meeting minutes, case histories, historical research, personal experience, you name it. The choice depends on the aspirations you have for building the authority of your book.

You face a new decision: What level of authoritativeness will you settle for? That is, what standard of research quality will you stake your reputation (and book) on?

Will you accept only peer-reviewed research? Will you limit testimony to eyewitnesses you consider reliable sources? Will you use only facts gathered during direct personal observation documented by onsite notes and photographs? Few people will limit their research to this degree. But the question is, What qualifies for bona fide evidence? Does Wikipedia cut it? How about popular magazines? Popular books by journalists? What about second-hand interview sources? Or sources with known conflicts of interest? How about people's recollections unchecked by documentary evidence?

One of the facts of the research life is this: As quickly as mice slip through the cracks of an old miner's cabin, distortions slip into the craniums of otherwise reliable people. An example: I once interviewed the former president of an organization about a board-of-directors' proxy fight. The fight, years earlier, was a defining moment in this man's civic life. At the fight's climax, he told me, he fended off a challenge to his control. He did so, in essence, by using the reservoir of his credibility to simply insist on the logic of his position—and the people challenging him backed down.

But the mice of time had gotten to his memory. In the board's archives, in minutes from the meeting—minutes he urged me to read—I discovered that not he, but the organization's incoming president, put down the challenge in just the way he described. My interviewee had projected onto himself the triumph of his successor-elect. To be sure, they were partners in the same effort. But the surprise—and lesson—was not that he was wrong. He was a man of impeccable integrity. It was that he had rewritten history in his own mind.

Leave aside the people who twist the truth knowingly. Even the trustworthy get it wrong. Honest Abes, even meticulous journalists, get fiction mixed with nonfiction all the time. I once phoned a man quoted in a premier business magazine known for its reliability. I asked him if he would tell me about a success a reporter credited him with, as I wanted to follow it up in more detail. He said the reporter had it all wrong. He had never even tried to do what he was credited with.

Caveat emptor. Researcher beware. Mistakes appear all the time in reputable magazines, even those who hire independent fact-checkers to verify quotes and anecdotes. So if you are reusing information you will not verify, recognize the pitfalls. More important, decide beforehand how much research risk you will take. What will you and won't you call fair game?

Be especially wary of taking testimony, facts, anecdotes, and stories from sources once removed from an event. We all learn the child's game of "phone"— with each telling, the message and facts go farther astray. Inconvenient caveats get left out. Convenient segues and rationales get invented. Dramatic actions get amplified. A reluctant, wishy-washy nobody gradually turns into a swashbuckling hero. It happens in print all the time.

A good rule of thumb: If a story or anecdote sounds too neat to be true, crosscheck it.

"Studies" and "surveys" require equal care before you cite them. Consider even the most reputable of publications: medical journals. Again and again, physician authors have been caught reporting "objectively" on treatments, while not revealing to their readers that they have a financial interest.

Perhaps the easiest mistake to make is to repeat "facts" you have learned to take as articles of faith. If you plan to repeat any content you're not absolutely sure of, check it out first.

Recall for example the famous letter by Chief Seattle written in 1854 as he ceded his lands to the United States: "How can you buy or sell the sky, the warmth of the land? The idea is strange to us. If we do not own the freshness of the air and the sparkle of the water, how can you buy them? Every part of the earth is sacred to my people. Every shining pine needle, every sandy shore, every mist..."

Quoted often, even in Al Gore's book, *Earth in the Balance,* the letter is a fake, written by a screenwriter in 1971.

Organize for just-in-time access

"I could have written that book." Have you ever heard that statement? Or thought it? If you're like me, you've probably read a book at some point and thought, Gee, that book's message is simple. It is clear. It is timely. Hey, anybody could write that kind of book.

But now you know how naïve that comment is. What people don't see in a book is all the work that went into making it "simple." The flailing around to refine a concept. The push to write a proposal. The late nights building a research trove. What people don't think about, in other words, is the hard part, the execution.

One of the hardest parts of execution, unappreciated by nonwriters, is organizing research. This is a task in book writing that has no parallel in short-form writing, whether articles, essays, white papers, or monographs. For short pieces, a mastery of several dozen documents and interviews suffices to produce content for a great piece of work. For books, you have to master hundreds or thousands.

While writing an article, I often let the papers cascade across my desk. I can rely on my memory to find whatever tidbit I need. But I never let a cascade build up when I do a book. The cascade would be suffocating.

Building on what you started in chapter 4, here's what I suggest adding to your book's paper trail, one chapter at a time:

EXPANDED ELECTRONIC DATABASE

EXPANDED MANILA FOLDERS

LOADED ELECTRONIC OUTLINE

The inventory of material you create for a book comprises thousands of research nuggets. A mother lode of nuggets. When you need to reach for one, you know you have a goldmine—but only if can lay your hands on the right nugget at the right time. That's why you need to arrange all the material in a storage-and-retrieval system.

On the market today are many kinds of software for taking, organizing, and searching notes. I don't give guidance on what works best. I use EndNote software and have tested only a few others. But you need to acquire your own means to quickly document, tag, and search all of your research.

Whatever software you use, tag your notes to mark them for individual chapters. You may also find it helpful to tag them with keywords relating to specific chapter messages. I can't stress this enough: Tag every document with a chapter. If, during book development, your chapter numbering changes, globally search and replace the former numbering.

Commit as much of your research as you can to electronic files. If you run across paper documents, add them to the manila chapter files created in chapter 4. Consider also scanning them into your electronic database. Don't create a slush pile for handling later—you'll never get to it. Decide which chapter every piece of material applies to, and put it in that file right away.

With your growing database and folders, you are ready for the final step: Loading your electronic outline. Your chapter and keyword tagging allow what seems like a feat of magic—calling up your database and querying it to give you just the material tagged for the chapter at hand. Bingo, all the documents you need appear in a neat list—and better yet, all the material you don't need remains hidden.

The next task seems arduous, but I find it's worth every minute. Read or skim every document for the chapter you're working on. Decide on the spot which lines and paragraphs in your notes are relevant. Cut and paste them into the note-taking level of your outline. As you do so, key into your outline where the excerpted text came from. Toggle back and forth between database and outline, pouring all your gold nuggets into the appropriate outline categories.

As you cut/paste your way through all the entries in your database, your chapter outline's word length will swell rapidly—probably reaching scores of pages. If you print it, you will probably regret it. Its beauty is not in print form. It is in allowing you, with a couple of mouse clicks, to "hide" the detail. Your top-level message outline still looks like a lean, finely wrought argument.

The loaded chapter outline is part of your just-in-time strategy. When you click to expose your research material, the nuggets sit right under the correct message or sub-message. When you start writing, you can grab them just as you need them. You no longer have to search through a landslide of paper. In fact, no papers are necessary on your desk. Remember to look in your manila files, of course, in case you have valuable nuggets there.

The word count of your chapter outline may zoom to tens of thousands of words. Although it will be unmanageable printed as a whole, you do want to print the skeletal view showing just the top-tier messages. Hang this skeleton above your desk. It is your road map. Meanwhile, all the detailed content will remain embedded right where you need it later on your computer.

An electronic system saves a lot of time even after you draft the manuscript. If your book has footnotes, endnotes, or bibliography, you'll face a formatting headache without software. With a good database program, you can create bibliographies in a few keystrokes. And if your editor questions a fact, you can search instantly to check it. Your loaded outline is the trail back to each chapter's original sources.

No job is more time-consuming after finishing a manuscript than having to double-check facts whose sources have slipped from your memory. Searches for the most trivial items can take hours. While it's hard to avoid this entirely, let your electronic system be your backup. Where your memory leaves off, your database begins.

With the loaded outline for each chapter, you are now ready to do what you thought writers did most of the time: write. That begins next, in the third step on the Road to Publication, Draft. First, though, take a last look at your loaded outline. Does it look well stocked with content? If needed, take an extra day to fill in the last gaps in your research.

YOUR PAPER TRAIL

STEP 10

✓ FULL ELECTRONIC DATABASE

✓ FULL PAPER FOLDERS

CHAPTER 11

WRITE

What is the secret to writing a manuscript efficiently? Not starting until you're ready. That's a key point of this book. Take time to get ready. Ready to write the right thing. Ready to write it in the right way. Ready to write with control.

For most authors, the time taken in getting ready adds up to much more than the time taken in writing. If you had imagined yourself, the writer, as turning into someone who spends most of your hours with fingers flying over the keyboard, think again. Composition takes less than one third of your time.

Paradoxically, the way to speed up writing is to resist getting started. Or more accurately, resist until you have a train of thought locked together and a train of cars brimming with content.

I periodically write before I'm ready, and I regret it. I've learned my lesson again and again but sometimes go astray anyway. I usually end up with a bunch of ill-conceived paragraphs in such a tangle I can't straighten them out. I learned my lesson first in my twenties, when a friend told me an article I had rewritten three times was unpublishable. I was too stubborn to hear the message at first, too embarrassed to deny it in the end. The reason was that I started too early.

If you're ready, a wonderful thing happens: Writer's block strikes far less often (if at all). Writer's block, in my experience, stems mainly from not knowing what you want to say. And not having an interesting way to say it. If you haven't filled your mind with worthy material—and sorted, organized, prioritized, and clarified it—you will find it hard to empty it cleanly onto the page.

I actually overstate to make a point. In truth, writing before you're ready can sometimes work wonders. The act of writing helps clarify thought. It primes the writing pump for pouring out words faster later. Writing to get ready is what I call "writing to think." If you're writing to think, you should think of yourself as journaling.

If you sense you need to engage in some writing to think, go back to your journal and experiment there. Or play around with words at the end of your electronic outline. But consider this writing-to-think throwaway work, doodles at the keyboard. It is akin to pencil work before you do the real thing—even though you may well find a pearl in the process.

But let's assume you're ready. With the thinking done, you've come to the moment you've been waiting for, actually moving ahead with the book manuscript. This is what I call "writing to deliver." You're now ready to write with control.

I recommend four tasks in this third step on the Road to Publication. Remember that you repeat these tasks for each chapter.

TAKE STOCK
DRAFT THE LEAD
DRAFT THE BODY
DRAFT THE CLOSE

Take stock

Just before you write, read your entire loaded chapter outline one more time. Think of this as loading the concept and content into your short-term memory. If, while reading, you notice a way to reorder things for better flow, do so. But focus foremost on absorbing material.

You don't need to separate good material from mediocre—although you can do so. (You should have left behind most of the mediocre stuff as you loaded your outline.) Just run the gold through your fingers. Your mind will start to naturally sift out the best stuff.

As you read, a fresh round of insights may emerge. You'll also naturally—and without a lot of effort—start to compose sentences in your mind. In fact, you can't reread your research and not imagine a few topic sentences, ponder transitions, or bubble over with new figures of speech. That's part of the benefit of rereading all your research.

This taking-stock process resembles opening a real warehouse full of your research, walking the aisles, and pulling out gems to put on a table. Consciously or unconsciously, you start to choose the best ones and organize them in patterns. In no time, you start to feel fully "ready."

Draft the lead

Start writing by drafting the lead and billboard to the chapter you're working on. If you're lucky (and smart), you will find that the text you drafted for the proposal's chapter summary will work just fine. Without extra effort, you're done. No anxiety about how to start. On the other hand, you may see right away that you have to take another crack. Use the craft tips for leads from chapter 6, Craft.

Leads and billboards have to hook reader interest, convey your message, orient the reader to your chapter's direction, and hint at drama and payoffs to come. With experience, you will want to jot down ideas for your lead for each chapter throughout the research process, instead of waiting until this point.

Good leads don't have to be complex, as you saw in chapter 6, but you should shoot above all for clarity. That is the highest virtue. Look at the lead to this chapter: simple and clear. If you use this kind of lead, the reader will always thank you.

If you use a long or complex lead, be sure it serves a purpose. One reason for a longer lead is to engage readers on more than one level—interest, intrigue, emotion. In a book by authors Ron Howard and Clint Korver, *Ethics for the Real World*, I advised opening a chapter with a story about an individual facing an ethical dilemma. In this case, we chose twenty-something Ali Hasan, an engineer.

The chapter opens by describing how Ali works in a company where the boss favors relatives in hiring. Ali is troubled by the nepotism. He thinks it hurts the quality of the

workforce, which of course, in turn, hurts everyone. Ali's story allows the lead to raise the question: Is nepotism in business ethical?

The anecdote allows Howard and Korver to accomplish the key purpose of an anecdotal lead—to illustrate and then segue to the chapter's message. The message is that people need to study their own personal and work lives to decide on ethical standards for themselves. Everybody needs to consider the issues that matter to them. Nobody can dictate standards to you. As for Ali, at the end of the lead, he decides nepotism is unethical.

The lead also accomplishes a second objective—it elicits empathy for another human being, and so holds the reader's attention. In fact, by raising an interesting question, using a personal anecdote, and completing a transition to the next part of the book's argument, the lead does double or triple duty. What's crucial, of course, is that the lead, with the related billboard, doesn't take the reader down a side road. It keeps the focus on the book's key question: How can Ali—or anyone—decide what is right or wrong?

Draft the body

With a lead and billboard done, draft the body of the chapter. This is the bulk of the writing work, but you'll find it much less tricky than a lead. The greatest danger is departing from your chosen argument and your specific outline points. This often happens when you get wrapped up in telling an anecdote—perhaps a story about the childhood of a character like Ali. In relating details that capture your fancy, you allow your focus to drift away from the details that support your book. Efficient writing demands that you remain vigilant: Control the content to serve your needs.

Draft the close

After laying down three to five messages in the body, close the chapter with a strong ending. As with leads, chapter closes take many forms, as discussed in chapter 6. Wrapping up with a sharp summary sentence is a good way to go. Clarity is a virtue. But look for a way to do more—with a hook, segue, zinger, cliffhanger, or other device. If possible, evoke wonder or spur insight.

As an example, Howard and Korver hooked back to Ali at the end of their chapter. That allowed them to bring closure to the Ali story. It also enabled them to express a deeper insight and provide a transition to the next chapter. Here's the very last part of the ending, with the authors reminding readers of how much soul searching people need to do to make ethical choices:

> Think back to Hasan...[who] quotes a famous Islamic Hadith as inspiration. "When asked, 'What is the major jihad?' the Prophet replied: 'The jihad of the self' (struggle against self)." And that is the struggle we continue in the next chapter.

When you finally put together the lead, body, and close for every chapter, you have advanced to a milestone on the path to publication: the rough draft (warts and all). To my mind, you have delivered the most important document in your book's paper trail.

The first complete pass can't be blemish-free. But if you look on the bright side, warts in your draft are actually a good sign. They testify to your not having let the small things distract you from getting the big thing accomplished: a complete document.

If your first pass is only 70 percent of the quality you wanted, this can seem discouraging. But take heart again. Most professional writers feel like gagging after the first pass. So if you've gotten to 70 percent, you've cleared a high hurdle—that's worth giving yourself praise—and you are well positioned to go the final 30 percent.

A word on discipline

People often remark that book authors must have a lot of "discipline." By that, they often seem to mean authors can force themselves to endure pain longer than anyone else. There may be some truth to that. But think of discipline another way, as not indulging in wasteful practices—practices you can learn to identify and avoid.

What's a wasteful practice? Stopping your writing to research a small detail—and so losing your train of thought. Writing way over your maximum word count—and so facing painful cuts later. Seeking perfection in one passage before moving onto the next—only to realize that the point you were polishing for hours wasn't quite the right point to start with.

When you're in the middle of writing, you'll have trouble identifying poor practices. But as an aid, here are some tips to efficient practices:

— Write when you're sharp: A pretty obvious pointer, but I mention it because it bears repeating. Write at the time of day when you think clearly and focus completely. I write best in the morning. I sometimes flail after 5:00 p.m. More than once I've had to throw out what I wrote late in the day, when I was dulled from eight hours of intense concentration.

— Resist early rework: Unless your first pass screams for it, don't stop to rewrite a passage that you think is passable. Go forward. Look in the rearview mirror only as needed to make sure you're building on material you've already put in the manuscript. If you know a passage needs repair, put a note in the text and come back after you finish the chapter.

— Course-correct often: This is a caveat to what I just said. If you realize you've gone down a side street with a Buddha and a tortoise, stop and back up immediately. Rewrite to keep on message. Sailors, lost at sea, usually sail in a circle. When you do this in writing, don't delay in righting your course.

— Focus on accuracy: As a corollary to resisting rework, don't labor over saying something elegantly once you're satisfied you've said the right thing. If you stated the concept correctly, push ahead. You can always come back to add elegance and color during an edit.

— Use placeholders: If you're missing a minor fact, or you know you can come up with a metaphor but can't think of it on the spot, don't open your browser and start researching. Journalists often put a "TK" (to come) in the text as a placeholder. Copy their example and come back to TKs later when your research won't interrupt your flow.

— Monitor your copyfit: Check the word count in each section as you write. Don't overshoot your guidelines by a wide margin. An anecdote may "deserve" more space, but don't let it run too long. You'll just end up throwing out good writing later.

— Stop for thumbnails: If you hit a wall, akin to writer's block, ask yourself, Have I finished thinking this through? Move from the keyboard back to a pencil. Outline your passage on the back of an envelope. A few bullet points on a scrap of paper can often crystallize a message and relieve the impasse.

— Dump the junk: Sometimes "good" content, once on the page, looks trite, cliché, or unauthoritative. You began with such high hopes for this juicy morsel, but on paper you find it unappetizing. You may not even understand why. Be quick to dump what your gut tells you doesn't "work."

— Watch the clock: If you've allocated a reasonable amount of time to write, stick with your plans. As you get near the deadline, your mind will often slash through the brambles quickly. Don't steal time from later chapters to feed earlier ones—unless you have a very good reason.

There are always exceptions. But writing to deliver demands that you make few of them. If you resist inefficient practices, you will move ahead faster. Your first pass may contain imprecise language. It may bristle with placeholders (TKs). It may stink with clichés. It may go on too long in some sections, not long enough in others. That's fine—so long as you're getting 70 percent of the way there.

In fact, that should be your goal—because that shows you've exercised discipline to compose efficiently. You may not have written anything you want to show anyone, but you now have something to work with. With your new grasp of the whole, when you finish all the chapters, you can more easily come up with precise language, fill gaps, and replace metaphors.

You also can perform writer's triage, allocating time first to the most critical problems in the whole book—not just the next problem you come across. When you write to deliver, you also preserve precious time to invest later in editing. For now, think of your work this way: You're building a house, and you will finish decorating all the rooms when the entire house is complete.

The rough draft of each chapter is always just that. Still, it's the biggest accomplishment in the book-development process. In the days before electronic documents, the rough draft meant reducing a pile of research papers a foot high to a chapter an eighth of an inch high. You could actually measure the progress with a ruler. It was impressive.

Today you can't measure the paper, but your progress is just as great. You have finished by far the hardest mental task in writing a book—creating the first cut of each primary chunk of the manuscript. You're now set to move ahead to the much easier task in the next chapter, step four in the Road to Publication, Edit and Beautify.

YOUR PAPER TRAIL

STEP 11

✓ROUGH DRAFT (WARTS AND ALL)

CHAPTER 12

EDIT AND BEAUTIFY

So now you have a rough draft with a lot of warts. What's the most efficient and effective way to edit out the warts? Rule number one: Don't start right away. Remember the Conservation of Freshness principle.

Freshness is a prerequisite for great editing. An absolute prerequisite.

As the old adage goes: If you can clearly see the problem, you are halfway to a solution. If you have refrained from reading your manuscript too many times, you will clearly see many, if not most, of its problems. And if you have taken a break after each draft, you have set yourself up with a sharp mind to edit the problems out of existence.

The most uncomfortable feeling in editing arises when you realize something in your text isn't right, but you can't figure out exactly what or why. That usually stems from over-familiarity. The more you labor over your text, the more thoroughly you inscribe your words and logic into your memory. The more you commit your words to memory, the more trouble you have shaking your mind out of its groove.

To make sure you're fresh after finishing each chapter's rough draft, take at least an overnight break, or better yet, a weekend away from home. Distract yourself with some activity to stop the text from running through your head like an endless tape.

I advise three editing tasks in this fourth step on the Road to Publication. Again, you repeat these for each chapter in your manuscript:

Edit the rough

Beautify the rough

Document sources

Edit the rough

You can edit a chapter by doing a "write through," editing line by line from the start. If you feel you laid down the paving stones of concept and content without bumps or gaps the first time around, this may be a good option. But usually a rough draft contains some broken if not overturned step stones, and doing a line-by-line edit draws you into fixing unimportant things.

Instead, I suggest editing selected parts of each chapter first. Start with the lead and billboard. If you haven't reread them too many times, you'll find them relatively easy to hone so that they reflect the precise direction of your chapter. Make sure they also engage the reader and carry the right message. A common mistake is a cryptic or ambiguous billboard.

Next, skim over your entire chapter. Does your message retain its integrity and continuity from one passage to the next? Examine each topic sentence, signpost, segue, or wrap-up sentence. Do they advance or adhere to your message plan? If your plan has evolved—it often does—revise your text to reflect the evolution.

Now check for balance. Are any sections long-winded? Do they get more weight than they are due? Mark sections that you need to beef up or pare down. While you're at it, fill in any big placeholders (TKs). The smaller TKs can wait if they distract you from larger edits.

Once you have finished this selective edit, line edit the entire chapter, paragraph by paragraph. Focus mainly on accuracy and precision. Make sure you say the right things in the right way. In other words, make sure the chapter "works." Here are some aids I find helpful:

— Edit when you're sharp: If you feel dull-witted, don't edit. You can easily make the text worse. You shouldn't drive when you're impaired, and you shouldn't edit, either.

— Practice triage: If something trivial reads poorly during the first pass, don't break your momentum to fix it. Mark your concern and move on. Save your fresh eyes for fixing the big problems first.

— Use freshness enhancers: If the text feels too familiar—that is, you can't discriminate between warts and beauty marks—read it aloud. Other aids: change the typeface or type size, read it in a public place like a bus station or park, read it to a loved one.

— Edit in context: Avoid the trap of getting overly focused on one faulty paragraph, so much so that you lose track of its place in the flow of the chapter. It's easy to spend an hour perfecting language in isolation only to find it doesn't work in context.

— Take three swings: If you realize you've lost your freshness in a particular passage, move on. Try three times to edit it, and if it's not right, quit. Your unconscious will work on it, and you can often come back later and easily make the repair.

Editing selectively is not natural. If you were to follow the path of least resistance, you would start at the beginning and write through the chapter. But the selective approach works better. It can save a lot of time because, by editing the high-level stuff first, you invariably change the treatment of entire chapter sections. Sometimes instead of rewriting passages you will then decide to delete them. No sense in line editing stuff you're going to throw away.

When you finish both the selective and the line edit on all your chapters, you've produced the next document in your book's paper trail: The rough draft with warts removed

Beautify the rough

Now that the chapter as a whole is in order, you're ready for a second editing phase. The text you have at this point is accurate and clear, but it is less than pretty. That is, you still don't have a draft you actually want to show anyone—or even print for yourself. You are still short of producing your best effort.

What you have so far probably contains colorless words. It sets forth fresh insights but in pedestrian ways. And despite your earlier efforts, you will decide it still uses too much abstract or overly conceptual phraseology. So it's time to beautify, that is, to inject into your writing wit, wisdom, and some of the wealth of the English language.

To beautify does not mean to ornament with adjectives and adverbs. Adding makeup, costume jewelry, or fashionable clothing cannot make an ugly or unfit body beautiful. Your job is to work on the musculature of the material, employing mainly nouns and verbs, to make the text more attractive and fit.

As before, take a break first. Start the beautification work after a weekend away from your book—and once your feeling of clarity has returned.

Then start with another round of line editing. Inspect the text sentence by sentence, leaving no word unexamined. Look for superfluous words and sentences, imprecise words and sentences, and ambiguous or abstract language. Substitute specific words or phrases for generalized ones. Redouble your efforts to replace the colorless prose with fresh words or figures of speech. If new words can help readers see, hear, smell, or feel what you're saying, use them.

Many books cover the fine points of editing in much more depth than this one has space for. (See Suggested Reading at the end of the book.) To my mind, though, the most powerful act in line editing is simple: unburdening readers of needlessly long sentences. Remember what some knowledgeable writer once said about the period: It rarely comes soon enough.

Cut words you can live without. Use more powerful verbs, more precise nouns. Break overloaded sentences into two (or three). Rephrase to express thoughts more compactly. Remove the verbiage remaining from early experiments in searching for the right way to say things.

An effort to shorten your sentences has several benefits. One is attacking long-windedness. Another is separating an amalgam of thoughts into separate, cleaner parts. When you draft something for the first time, you rarely figure out the most economical way to say it. Now ask yourself, How can the period come sooner?

Another thing about short sentences: People like them. They read them. Ever notice the sentences in ads? Shorter is better. A side benefit of brevity: It begets precision. Short sentences force vague words into the open.

Next, beautify your chapter with human stories. I find that most people— other than natural storytellers—unconsciously convert the events in life into concepts. This is natural. From experiences, stories, and daily life we draw lessons. Once we commit the lessons to memory, the specifics slip away. This process leaves most of us with less material than we think for effective writing. To write well, reverse the conceptualization. Pull the people back into the picture.

I was once collecting story material while traveling in Mississippi. In Clarksdale, in the cotton-growing Delta, I learned about how tight family connections were. This impressed me. Later, I looked for material that actually illustrated the point, and at first I didn't think I had any. Fortunately, I had captured some tidbits in a notebook. Among the best was a comment from a Mississippi woman: "They don't ask you what you do in Mississippi," she said, "They ask, 'Who's your Daddy?'"

Some book topics don't lend themselves to putting people in the foreground. But with effort, you can humanize even dry subjects. Think about financial journalists. They don't report just the fall in the U.S. dollar against other currencies. They explain what the fall means to consumers who buy tennis shoes or gasoline or French perfume. Likewise, good science writers don't just report on the size of the ozone hole or the intensity of UV rays. They find people with stories to tell about sunburn and melanoma.

You can do the same in big and small ways. If you're writing a business book, don't just say how business is changing. Say how the job of a specific person in a business has changed. Don't say China's increasing wage levels have driven up materials costs. Say they have pressured Jane Q. Purchase to bargain with new suppliers in Chengdu to hold down costs of imported steel. Put a person in the picture the reader can empathize with.

Finally, edit for insight. The whole point of a book is to reveal fresh insights for readers. Have you done so? Look at each of your points. Start with your billboard paragraph. Continue with those sentences where you state or hint at your insights, often at the beginning and end of sections. Can you improve your language?

When you've finished with these kinds of beautifying—for words, humanity, and insight—you should have your first print-quality document representing your manuscript. I call this the "first draft," or "first printable draft," because none of the previous, rough drafts was complete. The roughs lacked at least some content (TKs) .

Document sources

Now for housekeeping. To provide a way to trace your content back to its origin, document the source of everything in your text. Even if you have a great memory, you will not remember later where, in your trove of research documents from chapter 10, all your content came from. And if you forget later, and you need to lay your hands on a source to double-check a fact, you can expend hours of time. So cite the origin of all of your facts, figures, quotes, anecdotes, cases, testimony, and thoughts.

The best place for this documentation is in each chapter's footnotes or endnotes. I use the endnote function in my word processor. I do this as I write, and I can hide the endnotes after I enter them, so they don't clutter my screen while I'm writing. After I finish writing, I skim the entire document and add notes for anything else I think needs a source note. Often, in the rush of writing, I skip the citations, but I always come back to them before moving beyond the first draft.

If you're not going to include endnotes or footnotes in your published book, you should still make notes for yourself. Include specifics—titles, links, page numbers, Internet access dates, email dates, and locations of sources in the personal electronic and paper files you finished creating in chapter 10.

If you're going to include formal notes in your book, you don't need to edit them now. Just be sure you've captured the bibliographic data to make this easy later. You'll actually do a better job of editing footnotes when the book is done, when the text is final and you've cut passages you don't need. If you use bibliographic software, the computer will make it easy.

With your sources documented, you have finished a complete first draft of each chapter. If you haven't already, print the chapter. Now go on to write and edit the rest of the chapters. When you're done with all the chapters, written and edited one by one, you get to move back from a micro (chapter) focus to a macro (book) focus. That then readies you for the next, and fifth, step on the Road to Publication, Frame.

An important caution at this point. In the interest of the Conservation of Freshness principle, do not reread your chapter printouts without good reason. Save them only as a backup to your computer files. Then, when you come back to work on the chapters, you will return with reasonably fresh eyes. This will give you a huge advantage in bringing your manuscript up to 100 percent of its potential.

Though drafting all of the chapters in the book will take months, you will learn to view the long process as having a silver lining: You'll have time to forget what you wrote, or at least how you wrote it. You'll come back to the text of each chapter with some chance of reading it as if someone else wrote it. With a more objective eye, you'll have the power—and enjoy the pleasure—of editing with confidence.

YOUR PAPER TRAIL

STEP 12

✓ROUGH DRAFT, WARTS REMOVED

✓FIRST PRINTABLE DRAFT

CHAPTER 13

FRAME

The writing of a book is one long creative drama. Nothing is ever certain. At least it feels that way. The suspense goes on and on as you write each chapter: Will my idea work? Am I creating a decent manuscript?

It's hard to feel totally confident. You're working on your own. Nobody stands at your side to tell you you're doing the right thing. Alternative approaches keep floating through your mind. You sometimes go off course, run out of wind. In this intellectual marathon, you can wonder if all the evolving parts of your book will ever come together.

Well, sometimes they don't. At least not exactly the way you planned.

That's the nature of writing a book. In the ethereal world of ideas, you try to walk a steady path. But try as you may, the way ahead sometimes goes sideways on you. Your original vision doesn't quite fit the new curves, and you have to improvise. Mid-course corrections, seat-of-the-pants inventions, on-the-fly patches—you need them all to keep your project going.

And that presents a new challenge when you're finished with all the chapters. Given in-process adjustments that stemmed from your improvisation, you produced a manuscript that differs from your plan. Your messages have migrated to a new place. Maybe not a lot, but certainly some. Now you have to ask yourself: What do I do about it?

Answering this question brings you to the next phase in book writing, the fifth step on the Road to Publication. At this point, I suggest three tasks:

RECALIBRATE YOUR ARGUMENT

WRITE THE EPILOGUE

WRITE THE INTRODUCTION

Recalibrate your argument

For all your prewriting, outlining, and research work, the act of drafting a manuscript will still come as a process of discovery. As you discover things, you refine your plan, shifting your argument this way or that to improve its course. The more you discover, the more you shift. Eight, ten, or twelve chapters from the start, you find you have veered five, ten, or fifteen degrees from the original bearing.

This leads to the need for recalibration. You have created a misalignment between where you started and where you ended. The direction of not only your first and last chapters, but many of them in between, no longer syncs, and you need to get everything back in line.

To recalibrate, once you've finished your last chapter, you have to go back and amend the original guiding documents for your book—the message statement, title, table of contents, précis, and pitch. You don't need to actually produce new documents, but do mark them up with a pencil. Now that you've finished all the chapters, what have you discovered is your final direction? Capture this course-corrected argument on paper.

My experience in writing *Stairway to Earth* offers a good example of how the need for recalibration arises. When I started, I decided to write "a book about how to write a book." That seemed quite clear to me when I started out. And although that is still true, I gradually saw that my messages applied not to writing as in composing. They applied to process. That realization was especially helpful in deciding in later chapters what *not* to write about. It focused the book.

Write the epilogue

You might expect at this point that I would suggest you take your recalibration in hand and rewrite all your chapters. That will come soon. But first I suggest something else: creating your manuscript's bookends. Let's start with the epilogue.

You don't have to write a chapter to specifically close your book. If in your last chapter, you finished your argument, your book can end there. If you have more to say, or have loose ends to tie up, you probably want to write a closing. You can call it an epilogue, afterword, coda, conclusion, final thought, or anything else you like.

Even if you've finished what you had to say in the last chapters, consider the advantages of an epilogue. You can use it to interpret, amplify, hedge, footnote, or extend what you've already said. An epilogue can ignite a final few sparks of realization in your reader's mind. It can be a memorable sendoff.

You should ask: How might I end my book to give the reader some extra value? By reinforcing my main message? Recapping my argument's key points? Telling a last anecdote as a parting shot? Offering a story denouement? Discussing spin-off benefits from my insights? Raising new questions to ponder? Riffing on provocative, higher-level themes? Challenging or inspiring readers with a call to action?

Look at other books for examples. The last chapter in the classic, *The Inner Game of Tennis*, by W. Timothy Gallwey, starts this way:

> Up to this point we have been exploring the Inner Game as it applies to tennis. We began with the observation that many of our difficulties in tennis are mental in origin. As tennis players we tend to think too much before and during our shots; we try too hard to control our movements; and we are too concerned about the results of our actions and how they might reflect on our self-image. In short, we worry too much and don't concentrate very well...
>
> The key to spontaneous, high-level tennis...requires the learning of several inner skills, chiefly the art of letting go of self-judgments...
>
> Not only can these inner skills have a remarkable effect on one's

forehand, backhand, serve and volley (the outer game of tennis), but they are valuable in themselves and have broad applicability to other aspects of life.

Gallwey titles his epilogue, "The Inner Game Off the Court." He calls it a chapter, but it specifically provides a bookend to his argument about tennis. He uses this bookend to show how his thoughts on tennis apply to everyday life, specifically, to the handling of stress. By including this close, Gallwey chose a common way to finish a book: Suggesting to the reader the broader implications of a book's main argument.

The epilogue of my book, *Nature's Keepers: The Remarkable Story of How the Nature Conservancy Became the Largest Environmental Organization in the World,* starts this way:

> Victor Shelford had a simple, universal yearning: to have an impact, to make his mark. He wanted to change the world—for everyone's good. If he succeeded, if he unleashed a chain of events and the energies of other people, the University of Chicago ecologist could have an effect for generations.
>
> But fulfilling his yearning would not come easily. At fifty-eight years of age, the pioneer in the field of ecology watched as the organization he had founded back in 1915, the Ecological Society of America, voted to forbid one of his favored programs: taking action to protect natural areas. The society couldn't even write a congressman to urge saving a virgin forest.
>
> As the society voted in 1946 to abolish the subgroup he'd started in 1917, Shelford fostered a schism. He and fourteen others, including three past presidents, signed a proposal to form a new group to take direct action to *protect* ecosystems. On the other side stood partisans of tradition, society members who would stick with scholarship, the *study* of ecosystems.

In this case, I used the epilogue to add a thought the book did not contain. Shelford illustrated the huge role of many "unsung heroes" in making the Nature Conservancy a success. Bringing in his story allowed me to also answer an expected objection by readers—that I had left out key players in my narrative.

Once you recalibrate your argument, you'll have a good feel for the things that should come in your epilogue. Other worthwhile items might include material covering unanswered questions, unmet promises to your reader, nagging caveats, omitted gems of content, messages that deserve more limelight, and orphan message points that need a good home.

Outline your epilogue like any other chapter. It should have a single message, however. Decide what you want to accomplish and stick with it. Often, under the umbrella of one final point, you can achieve several things. For example, you might be able to summarize your key takeaways, raise new questions, inspire your readers with another insight, and issue a call to action—so long as you position all of this material to serve the umbrella message.

Keep your epilogue to no more than half the length of your main chapters. If you have to leave something essential out, you can always write a postscript, author's note, or similar add-on. Don't include material that takes away from your epilogue's integrity. It should end your book in a focused way.

Write the introduction

Some truths have to be experienced to be believed. One of them is this: Not until you've finished your last chapter are you qualified to write your introduction (or preface or prologue).

To be sure, when you start your book, you *think* you know what you want to say. And you *should* know. But truth be known, you're actually only certain about what you wanted to say when you're finished writing.

This idea may run counter to your natural urge to begin at the beginning. But only after recalibrating your message, and writing your epilogue, can you pin down your introductory message precisely. The payoff for waiting will be a much more cogent, articulate, and interesting introduction. And it will be easier to write as well.

The first lines of your introduction are key. They often sway bookstore readers (including online readers) to either buy or reshelve your book. So write your first words only when you're sure you have them pegged. Here's how Jon Franklin, the journalist who wrote *Writing for Story: Craft Secrets of Dramatic Nonfiction by a Two-Time Pulitzer Prize Winner,* began his preface:

> As a young man desperately committed to literature, I restlessly searched my local libraries for a book that would reveal to me The Secret of Writing.
>
> I looked especially hard for books by bona fide professional writers. Whenever I found one I always rushed right home with it and, with flushed face and pounding heart, read it through from cover to cover.
>
> I loved such books. I was always delighted with the easy, swaggering way the writer took me into his confidence. I identified with him as he described his early rejection slips (Oh, I knew, *I knew!*), and chuckled as he described his agonies over writer's block and his exploits in the dark and dangerous jungle of publishing. Ah, yes, it is a writer's lot to suffer.
>
> Yet as sincerely as I appreciated the writers who shared their war stories with me, I somehow always reached the end of the book before they got around to revealing The Secret.

Franklin then crystallized the message of his book in remarkably familiar concept: Revealing "The Secret" to performing a difficult task. He was able reduce his main message to such simple language because he wrote the preface *after* he wrote the rest of the book (and because he writes exceedingly well). As an aside, Franklin, a celebrated teacher of literary journalism, advises writers to draft all narrative stories backwards: Write the most important part, the climax, first, and then write everything else to align with it.

Introductions come in many forms. In concept, how-to, self-help, and similar books, introductions do three things: They pique the reader's interest or emotion. They explain why your target audience would want to read the book. And they give background to prepare the reader for what's to come.

To pique reader interest, an introduction should start with a strong lead, built the same way as a lead in any chapter. Don't be fancy unless you have a good reason. If your reader already yearns for answers, get right to the point. Whatever you do, make sure the lead makes readers thirst for more. It should drive them on to the next part of the introduction, where you show and tell why your book is worth reading.

Recall the marketing sections in your book proposal. Touch on the same points in the introduction, phrased to address your readers instead of publishers. Among the points to include: a summary of your messages and argument; how your book stands out from others; what your book offers that's new; why the book is relevant today; what your experience and credentials are; what benefits readers will enjoy; what worthy content you will share.

Think of the introduction as a promise to the reader. It tells people what you will deliver. To your targeted readers, the promise should be irresistible. Your book is a key for a lock they have yearned to open for a long time.

Many writers hesitate to give away their argument in the introduction. They think concept books, like narrative nonfiction or novels, should create suspense. But being cagey will just annoy your readers. Recall those full-page ads for drugs, gadgets, or self-help courses to improve your love life. They promise untold benefits but never tell you what you're getting. Don't follow their example.

As Susan Rabiner and Alfred Fortunato say in their excellent book, *Thinking Like Your Editor*, "Spill the beans!" Preview your best thoughts.

Remember to include in your introduction any background your reader will need to get oriented. For example: What prompted you to write the book? What parts of your field are you not covering? What caveats apply to your opinions? What are the boundaries of your research? Since this kind of information often makes dull reading, try to work it into the flow of the introduction's text rather than making a separate section.

End your introduction with a strong close, just like any other chapter. Some readers (and writers) consider introductions as throwaways. Who in a hurry reads them? But keep book browsers in mind. Plan to convince them that your book will make lively, insightful, and companionable company from the first page to the last.

With the introduction complete, you finally have a complete draft of your book. The paper trail you started weeks before, with the message statement, has led you step by step to a full manuscript. Hats off to you. If you're inclined to celebrate key milestones, put your computer in sleep mode (after doing your backups) and celebrate.

What you have written, of course, is utterly unpublishable. All first drafts are. But having written all your chapters, and having framed your book with bookends, you can feel an incredible sense of control of the process. You are certain to be on the road to finishing an excellent manuscript. What's next are the final iterations to hone your writing—much easier than getting it down in the first place. And that's the subject of the next chapter and final step on the Road to Publication, Bounce and Bounce Back.

YOUR PAPER TRAIL

STEP 13

✓EPILOGUE

✓INTRODUCTION

CHAPTER 14

BOUNCE AND BOUNCE BACK

It takes a big ego to write a book. How else could you presuppose so many people would want to hear what you have to say? But it also takes the ability to set that ego aside if you want to turn a first draft into a superb final one.

No matter how fresh your eyes, other people's eyes are a lot fresher. You need to take advantage of them. Check your ego and ask friends and colleagues to read your book and offer help and criticism. And be ready to take the bad news —and not just take it with a stiff upper lip. Take it to heart.

Your job from here to the end is simple compared to what you've done so far: Take what you have and, draft by draft, improve it. Use the feedback you get to revise the manuscript until it is just right. I advise four tasks in this last phase in producing a manuscript:

BOUNCE

EDIT

BOUNCE AGAIN

POLISH

Bounce

Over the months you've been working on your book, friends and colleagues have probably asked you many times: How's the book going? After answering with a status update, you should always be ready with a question of your own:

Would you review a draft for me when it's done?

Few favors need asking more than this one. You desperately need an independent review of your manuscript. Your editor remains your most important reviewer. After all, he or she bought your idea, fought for acceptance of it inside the publishing house, and has coached you along the way. In fact, your editor may have asked to read early drafts, and may have even read all the chapters to help you recalibrate your direction.

Still, you need to ask others to help you out. Songwriter Bill Jonas has an interesting way to approach this task. After he writes a song, he gives it to people he classifies as "first responders," "second responders," and "third responders." He figures most writers need all three.

First responders say, Wow! You created something! They don't express criticism, but instead appreciation. They are the people who have unconditional positive regard for your work. People like your mother. Their compliments give you confidence.

Jonas next asks the second and third responders. The second responders tell him what they like and what he can improve. They offer constructive criticism. Third responders are the ones who don't mince words. They say, Yes, that's a keeper! Or, No, that's a loser. If you go to them with a product lovingly created, and they don't like it, their comments are likely to make you squirm and fret.

Think of Jonas's taxonomy when you ask people to look at your draft. First responders are always helpful in keeping your spirits up—which can make your writing better. But be sure to get feedback of the other two kinds. You're not going to find your weaknesses and blind spots on your own. As many engineers say when they're trying to improve something, "Problems are good. No problem is a big problem."

Before you send out your first draft, be sure it represents your work accurately. If your recalibration showed you were especially wide of the mark, be sure you've adequately rewritten the wayward chapters. You might need to complete a second draft of the manuscript if the first remains rough. No sense in sending out a broken product and having people point out the obvious to you.

The time for humility comes when you get comments back. Be prepared for people pointing out mistakes and weaknesses in even your favorite passages. It's easy to reject comments you don't like. And when you get all that red ink back, you'll probably agree with H. G. Wells, when he said, "No passion in the world is equal to the passion to alter someone else's draft." (The more red ink you get, the more you'll agree with him.)

But remain receptive to bona fide criticisms, even as you put them in perspective. One factor to keep in mind is the varying depths of your reviewers' readings. You'll want to ask: How discriminating were they? Did they breeze through the draft or read it as closely as they would their own writing?

I learned as a magazine editor that I couldn't properly comment on, or edit, an article, until I had read it three times. On the first read, I marked what didn't work for me, even if I didn't understand why. On the second, with knowledge of the whole piece, I could figure out why things didn't work. On the third, I could finally figure out what the writer was trying to do. And that's when I could start editing.

If your reviewers read your draft superficially, they may have only marked what didn't work for them, without saying why. Still, that's a big help right there, even if they didn't understand what your aims were or how to help. If they took issue with a concluding sentence, for example, ask: Is the problem the sentence, the setup, the context, or something earlier in the argument? When someone marks something, although they may not have marked the source of the problem, they usually reveal that you do have a problem of some kind.

One thing to watch for: Reviewers may presume goals for your book different from yours. If they think your manuscript should be the definitive work on the subject, for example, look out! They may say you're oversimplifying, misconstruing points, and omitting coverage of key ideas, context, people, case studies, and so on. The real problem may be that you didn't state clearly the boundaries of your argument in your chapter or in your introduction. (Or then again, maybe you promised more than you delivered.)

Edit

After you get over all the red ink from reviewers, decide what you will and won't do. This will be your rewrite plan, probably a chapter-by-chapter list of changes. Your editor will send you a memo that details changes, along with a marked-up manuscript. Combine these in your action list.

If you're lucky, your rewrite plan will amount to no more than a lot of line editing. More often, you'll need to restructure a few passages, probably whole chapters. If your revision plan calls for big changes, don't try to edit on screen. Print each chapter. Arrange pages on a table, one beside the other. Look at the whole chapter, every passage in view. Assess what your overall actions should be.

With the chapter laid out, edit in the same way you did last time, for your first draft. Look first at leads and billboards. Skim from one topic or signpost sentence to the next. Check transitions, hopping from one paragraph to the next. Mark how you want to move things around. With a sweep of the eye, you can see how you need to rearrange any text that is out of place.

Once you're happy with your plan, do the edits on your computer. Then go back to the beginning and line edit for flow, words, humanity, and insight, just as in the last chapter. Although you are creating the second draft, go through the chapter several times so you have read every passage in context. On the last pass, read it aloud. If it helps you to read more attentively, change or enlarge the typeface.

On this second draft, you'll appreciate the Conservation of Freshness Principle. If you haven't reread your writing since drafting, you'll feel clearheaded during the line editing. The awkward, superfluous, and silly passages will stand out. All the broken logic will shout for repair, and you'll be able to fix things in seconds you struggled with on the first draft. If you're like me, you'll wonder how you wrote such illogical stuff.

Remember to persist with your efforts to stay fresh, even now that you're becoming very close to your text. Refrain from rereading the text unless you have a specific editing task. Conserve whatever drops remain in your reservoir of freshness for the third draft.

Bounce again

Once you're done with the second draft, send it to reviewers again. Or if you're confident about your changes, send just the passages you would like to double-check. You can ask only so much of friends and colleagues. So make sure you first ask for feedback on chapters or passages that have given you the most grief. (If you were confident enough that you could edit your first draft without help, now you can tap your friends for the first time.)

Again, your editor will be your first and most important judge, but at this point neither he nor she may have fresh eyes, either. Then, too, editors have a lot of projects other than yours, so they may not give you a second – or third-responder's level of constructive criticism this time around.

Whether you send out the entire manuscript or not, and even if your reviewers return it quickly, let some time pass before you work on it for your third draft. Without some time, you can't possibly recover a sense of freshness. Leave at least a week. The more time you can let the manuscript sit after the last reading, the better the final product will be.

One issue to bear in mind during this last edit: A lot of time has passed since you proposed your book. Ask yourself: How much has changed in my subject area? Have the terms of discussion evolved? Are my message and language still current? What do I foresee will be the likely shape of the world when the book comes out?

When Marc Epstein and I wrote *Counting What Counts: Turning Corporate Accountability to Competitive Advantage,* we made a simple argument: Managers of companies that measure, publicly report, and in turn improve their performance will out-compete all others. During the last draft, we noticed people increasingly referring to the practices we advocated as "transparent." To be current, we introduced the term in our manuscript in several places. (Inevitably, ten years later, "transparency" has moved from current to cliché.)

If you want your book to sound up-to-date, consult Google Zeitgeist about the ebb or flow of current terms. On the flip side, cut terms and tidbits that have the opposite effect. Dated or outdated material is a turnoff. If you're writing about corporate crime and your accused embezzler clears his name, find another slouch to lampoon.

Polish

Sort through all the comments you get on your manuscript and create a second rewriting plan. Use the same editing process you used for the second draft to improve your text. Refine the high-level messages first. Polish everything else second. Then do a complete line edit.

No book should require fewer than three printable drafts. Even at the last draft, you will be amazed at the foolishness you find. If you read it aloud, overused words will stand out like echoes in an empty room. If you have people read questionable passages to you, they will stand out even louder.

Don't be surprised if, at the eleventh hour, you realize a much better way of saying something. The relentless approach of the final deadline, and the reality of going into print, forces you to dig deeper for the best your mind can produce. Don't let yourself tinker endlessly at this point, though. Perfection is the enemy of completion. Format the manuscript for the copyeditor and hit the send button. You still have another set of eyes to catch weaknesses.

Hitting the send button should give you a great feeling. If you've had yourself on a work regimen dictated by a relentless writing schedule, you've just freed yourself from bondage. If you got an advance, you're about to be paid the balance. Many housekeeping tasks remain, but you've just completed the final step on the Road to Publication. You've put your lifework into the hands of your publisher.

This is the real deal. And whatever work remains, you have plenty of reason to celebrate (again). Don't wait for publication to pat yourself on the back, as that's a long ways off, six to nine months. Celebrate, because you've successfully managed your way through the book-writing process, and you have produced a piece of writing that will make you an author—something that most people just dream about.

YOUR PAPER TRAIL

STEP 14

✓SECOND DRAFT

✓DELIVERED MANUSCRIPT (THIRD DRAFT)

AFTERWORD

AFTER YOU FINISH

When it comes to writing a book, there are many endings and beginnings. You end message development, you start the outlining. You end the outlining, you start writing. You end the first draft, you start the second. Each ending marks a triumph over a significant chunk of work. And along with each triumph goes a deliverable, a document you can point to as showing you have achieved a milestone.

One of the last milestones is the finished manuscript. And that's where the guidance in this book ends. With the next beginning, "production," your work moves into the hands of a team comprising editor, copyeditor, production manager, designer, proofreader, indexer, and so on. The team shepherds the manuscript from an electronic file to a book. You're part of this team, but you're not the leader.

The change in leadership could bother you, especially if you are sensitive to every detail in your book. But it probably will also come as a relief. You can sit back and let the burden fall on someone else to tell you what to do next—even as you keep your eyes wide open for holdups and mishaps.

Here's what you can expect as the production team gets going: The copyeditor will make sure every sentence makes sense and minds the rules of English. Expect to learn a few things when you get the copyeditor's marked-up manuscript back. He or she will have lots of questions. Did you really mean the largest hailstone every recorded was seventeen inches in *diameter?*

Next the team will prepare pages, or "proofs," of the book. You'll get to review them and insert marks of your own. The proofs look just like photocopies of the actual book pages. Following the pages, the team will send you index text, cover text, flap text, and somewhere along the way, various text for marketing.

You still have some housekeeping chores before the team prepares the final proofs. Your to-do list might read something like this: Write the acknowledgments. Edit the endnotes. Prepare the bibliography or references. Fact-check quotes, numbers, anecdotes, testimony, case stories. Solicit permissions to re-publish copyrighted material. Ask for jacket endorsements.

None of this work is hard, but like the laundry, it can pile up. Be sure to budget some time for it.

When the production team finishes every page—when it enters final changes from you and the proofreader, and outputs a complete set of digital pages for the printer—the production ends. This kicks off another beginning, the ramping up of promotion. Once again, your publisher will take the lead, preparing pre-launch publicity. You should plan, however, to step back in as a partner—and even be ready to take the lead again when the time is right.

Promotion can involve quite a few tasks. It may include book signings, radio/TV appearances, speeches, workshops, video trailers, website production, blog posting—just about anything you can dream up. The scope of these tasks often comes as a surprise to a new author. Although the book-writing process is done, your job as the author goes on and on. The publisher does not do all, or even most, of these tasks.

Calling an end to the promotion phase is really up to you. At what point do you feel you have given your child the care, feeding, and support needed to realize its potential? After three months? Three years? If you publish a best seller, your publisher will stick with you and help with support for years. But, failing that, how much more time and money will you spend?

Eventually, you'll probably wind down your support for a book, and then the question arises: Will I write another?

Whatever you decide, at least you now know what you're getting into. You know how to descend the Stairway to Earth—delivering the précis, pitch, positioning journal, proposal, and all the other prewriting documents. You also know how to travel the Road to Publication—delivering research, outlines, and first, second, and third drafts.

You know, too, that if you break the book-writing process into pieces, it won't break *you* into pieces. You can build a strong argument, sell it to a publisher, pace yourself during writing, and celebrate a manuscript adeptly completed. You're no longer an author in training. You're a professional.

SUGGESTED READING

The shelves of the world's bookstores are filled with great books on nonfiction writing. I can't list even a fraction of the worthwhile ones. So I've chosen just one each from a handful of useful categories.

My favorite on writing serious books:

Rabiner, Susan, and Alfred Fortunato. *Thinking Like Your Editor.* New York: W. W. Norton & Company, 2002.

On structuring an interesting article (or chapter): Blundell, William E. *The Art and Craft of Feature Writing.* New York: Plume (Penguin), 1986.

On writing narrative nonfiction: Franklin, Jon. *Writing for Story.* New York: Plume (Penguin), 1986.

On the basics you should never forget: Strunk, William Jr., and E. B. White. *The Elements of Style.* New York: Macmillan, 1979 (multiple editions).

A classic on a variety of craft: Zinsser, William. *On Writing Well.* New York: HarperCollins, 1976.

The classic reference work for books: *The Chicago Manual of Style.* Chicago: University of Chicago Press, 2010 (16th edition).

For inspiration and commiseration on the writing life: Lamott, Anne. *Bird by Bird.* New York: Anchor Books (Doubleday), 1994.

ACKNOWLEDGMENTS

As a first job in the 1970s, I took a position as editor of two hiking-trail guidebooks. The books were about the Appalachian Trail, the two-thousand-mile footpath from Georgia to Maine. I had no publishing qualifications. A former boss (thanks, Bob) set me up, because I had worked on trails for many summers.

So I'm especially indebted to those who taught me writing, editing, and publishing on the job. Everything I know comes from working, not from a degree in writing. Over thirty years ago, a Library of Congress editor, Florence Nichol, copyedited my first two guidebooks. That was Florence's way of teaching me everything I should already have known, which I hadn't learned as a biology major.

Years later, I learned about commercially published books from an expert, Donna Carpenter, whom I want to thank for getting me into the business. Donna ran the celebrated Wordworks book-packaging business in Boston, and in the 1990s trusted me to draft part or all of a number of books. Although Donna didn't document her process, she knew how to produce a best seller, and I absorbed a lot from her example.

Donna had many talented people working for her. One of them was Erik Hansen, whose support, friendship, and publishing insights I've valued over many years. Working in partnership with Donna was Helen Rees, now my agent for many years. Thank you, Helen, for never mincing words on how to deliver proposals that sell.

In my years in the business, I've worked with many editors at publishing houses, and each one has taught me new things about the business. Thanks to Nick Philipson, Marnie Cochran, Allison Brunner, Johanna Vondeling, Donya

Dickerson, Jacque Murphy, and Laurie Harting.

Two writing colleagues read drafts of this book and gave me comments. Thanks to Lee Burnett and Andy Dappen for helping me make the book much better. I'm privileged to have such loyal friends. Lauren Byrne copyedited the entire book. Thank you, Lauren, for the first-class work.

Many fellow writers, writing-conference speakers, writing teachers, and above all, consulting clients have contributed to my knowledge and experience. Like any author, if I appear to have anything intelligent to say, it's only because I'm standing on other people's shoulders. I would especially like to cite the influence of Jon Franklin, a two-time Pulitzer Prize winner and longtime teacher who, with wife Lynn, runs the Writer-L discussion group. When it comes to explaining systematic ways to tackle the writing process, Jon has no peer.

Thanks finally to my wife, Sue, who patiently listens to each of my latest brainstorms about how to write more effectively. In my first salaried job (and hers), she could see I was short on writing qualifications. She loaned me a copy of Strunk and White's *Elements of Style,* a bible for writers. I've kept the book on my shelf ever since, a bible, a totem, a keepsake, a memento of Appalachian romance, and of course I have no plans to return it.

INDEX

ABOUT THE AUTHOR

Bill Birchard is a writer, author, and book consultant based in Amherst, New Hampshire. He has been writing books and articles for thirty years. Since the mid-1980s, he has written about business, management, the environment, and self-help. Formerly editor of *Enterprise*, a magazine for executives, his articles have appeared in *Fast Company, CFO, Chief Executive,* and *Strategy+Business.*

His most recent book is *Merchants of Virtue* (Palgrave Macmillan, 2011), the story of one company's twenty-year journey to sustainability. Other books include *Nature's Keepers* (Jossey-Bass, 2005), *The One-Minute Meditator* (Perseus, 2001), with David Nichol, and *Counting What Counts* (Perseus, 1999), with Marc J. Epstein.

Birchard's work as a consultant includes *Ethics for the Real World* by Ronald Howard and Clint Korver (Harvard Business Press, 2008), *Wal-Smart: What It Really Takes to Profit in a Wal-Mart World* by William Marquard (McGraw-Hill, 2007), and *The Discipline of Market Leaders,* a *New York Times* best seller authored by Michael Treacy and Fred Wiersema (Perseus, 1995).

Birchard's long experience with the challenges of book writing has led him to develop a process to initiate, guide, and reliably deliver manuscripts. He continues to apply that process for his own byline, as a ghostwriter, as a book-proposal writer, and as a book-writing coach.

BILLBIRCHARD.COM

STAIRWAYTOEARTH.COM

CPSIA information can be obtained at www.ICGtesting.com
Printed in the USA
BVOW081038030413

317114BV00002B/137/P